Little Did I Know

An Anthology on Loving and Companioning Young Lives

EDITED BY VANESSA RUSH SOUTHERN

Skinner House Books
Boston

skinnerhouse.org

Printed in the United States

Cover design by Nelly Murariu
Text design by Tim Holtz
Author photo by Rohit Menezes

print ISBN: 978-1-55896-886-8
eBook ISBN: 978-1-55896-887-5

5 4 3 2 1

26 25 24 23 22

Cataloging-in-Publication data on file with the Library of Congress

"Fertile Dreams" by Vanessa Rush Southern is adapted from *Miles of Dream* (Skinner House, 2015).

"Two Pink Lines" by Kate Landis is adapted from *Stubborn Grace* (Skinner House, 2020).

"A Friendly's Ice Cream Baby" by David O. Rankin is adapted from *Portraits From the Cross* (Skinner House, 1978).

"To Life Ordained" by Jane Rzepka is adapted from *A Small Heaven: A Meditation Manual* (Skinner House, 1989).

"Love's Pronoun Is Plural" by Elea Kemler was previously published in Braver/Wiser, uua.org/braverwiser, July 19, 2017.

"Another, Truer Song" by Elea Kemler was previously published in Braver/Wiser, uua.org/braverwiser, February 21, 2018.

"Carried Up to Bed" by Elizabeth Lerner Maclay is adapted from *Falling into the Sky*, ed. Abhi Janamanchi (Skinner House, 2013).

Contents

Introduction

I have one kid, one great kid, one kid who is getting close to leaving home. I have a kid who came into the world with the help of some gifted and deeply humane doctors (thank you, RMA of New Jersey and Dr. Michael Drews, in particular). I found a therapist who, as grace would have it, had been through infertility herself and was a leader in the national infertility organization, Resolve (blessings upon you, Dr. Nancy Gera-Moglia). Rohit and I were determined to be parents, however life would allow, but the journey was harder than we had imagined.

The pain challenged us and it changed us. Losing pregnancies after Leila was born, I found solace in thinking of myself as offering parenting to the world. Currently, and for the second time, we have a nephew coming to live with us, so life is cooperating with our invitation. And the journey through infertility made me more aware of all the non-normative stories in this piece of our lives—of the choices we are presented with and make, of where life-nurturing-young-life can take us or not.

For myself, it has been one big humbling and wisdom-making adventure. Little did I know how much the journey into and through parenting would involve constantly stepping into the unknown. Little did I know how often I would be challenged to hold the spiritual stance of embracing the unfolding of life on its own terms and timelines, the holding of heartbreak (yours and theirs), the delight in surprises (yours and theirs), and the seemingly eternal necessity of learning as you go. And little did I know how much parenting would be like looking at a mirror held up to show me the best and worst of myself, how much this life would ask me to step into my best as often and as faithfully as possible, and how much I would learn from Leila about how to be fully, gorgeously human.

Love is a crucible for change and the impetus to change. You and I do for love what we would not do for almost anything else. For those we love we rise to the occasion (all occasions), trying to be what and who they need us to be, reaching for all the arrows in our quivers and treasure in our chests in order to try and do so, be so. Little do we know, when we commit to love someone, especially a young child or youth, how it will change us and how much it will demand of us.

Which brings me to now: Leila, my daughter, is seventeen and will be leaving home soon. Perhaps you are good at goodbyes. I am not. As Edna St. Vincent Millay famously wrote, "I am not resigned," but I need to be mature when the time comes. So I thought that this project would help. A chance to gather up stories and the wisdom that others have found and forged in this part of their life's journeys, to help me reflect on my own. To try and wrap a bow around it. An anthology that is a ritual of goodbye.

The pieces included are all deeply personal and vastly different. Some of the writers included in the collection chose to be parents and some didn't. Some chose not to be parents for a time and chose differently later in life. There are aunts and uncles and the family we choose, grandparents, single parents, divorced parents, bereaved parents, ministers—a spectrum of experience offered by people reflecting on the roles children and young people have played in their lives and in their larger search for meaning.

I hope you see yourself and your experience reflected in some of the stories. If you don't, or just have a story to add, I invite you to send it to me at vrsouthernbook@uusf.org. Maybe we'll start a larger library of reflections and gathered-up wisdom about this piece of life.

This book is dedicated to Naomi Nirmala Mascarenhas e Menezes, my mother-in-law and a fierce and loving mother, grandmother, auntie, and friend to so many. She passed away in October of 2021, leaving a huge legacy of love in her wake. And to Bean, who, as my mother would say, chose us, and thank goodness she did. The world got a whole lot sweeter one night not so long ago.

With blessings for the ways we love the world forward,

Vanessa Rush Southern

A Season of Advent . . . and Authentic Beginnings

MANISH MISHRA-MARZETTI

As a child, I wanted to grow up and be the Old Woman Who Lived in a Shoe—because, of course, having a gazillion kids in one's life, with a giant shoe as a romper room, sounded positively superb! But, more deeply, this children's rhyme also captured the longing for parenthood that has always resided in my heart. There was just one obstacle to making this vision (or some version of it) a reality: the fact that I am gay, and therefore the culturally typical route to parenthood, via biological procreation, was unlikely.

Decades later, in 2010, my husband and I held this longing together as we entered the open adoption process. As we did so, our participation in mandatory adoption orientations brought to light for us the profound and very personal heartache that some heterosexual couples and individuals experience prior to arriving at adoption. Our journey was different: biological procreation was out, *prima facie*, and we did not have the financial resources to consider surrogacy. We were truly thrilled at the prospect of open adoption: this was our first-choice route to parenthood.

As a part of the open adoption matching process, couples and individuals approved for adoption prepare a brief electronic profile, which includes a summary of the prospective family's adoption criteria and personal background, as well as a longer, more detailed "portfolio," which is basically the prospective family putting its best foot forward in sharing with a birth mom who they are and the environment they would offer a child. Birth mothers review these materials and then choose which family to place their baby with. Our portfolio included a video message to birth moms, an electronic collage of photos of my husband and me, and short descriptions of the life we had built together. We talked about my husband's paid work in retail sales of high-end cosmetics, as well as his deeper calling as an artist; we described my diplomatic and ministerial careers and my commitment to community, locally and globally. We shared our intention to raise our child within the open, liberal values of Unitarian Universalism: of having "uncles," "aunties," "grandparents," and peers within the extended family of the congregation. Our portfolio was a view into us; it was our prayer, our longing, given shape and voice.

After completing all these and other requirements, a prospective family then waits . . . and typically waits some more. Occasionally, an adoption comes through within days or weeks, but it is not unusual for some adoptive families to wait for even a couple of years. The Christian tradition refers to the time before Christmas as Advent, because it is a time of anticipatory and prayerful waiting. Such was the season that my husband and I now entered, one of mostly silent anticipation, with all the routines of day-to-day life continuing, as if we were not on the verge of something momentous. This quiet waiting was, however, occasionally interrupted when the adoption agency would reach out to us when a set of circumstances closely, but not fully, matched our adoption criteria. "Would you like this birth mother to consider you, alongside other potential families?" was invariably the question, to which we always enthusiastically responded, "Yes."

At first, these calls were exciting! They were our only tangible indication that we were under active consideration. Yet, after hearing nothing further in the ensuing days, we would piece together the conclusion that the birth mother had selected another prospective family. This realization was always an immense letdown, and yet unavoidably one possible outcome of the process. As the months wore on, we received so many of these calls (typically one or two a month) that we knew that plenty of birth mothers were actively considering us . . . just, none of them were choosing us to place their child with. Discouragement began to emerge. In the early months of 2011, we had a one-month period in which we received four such calls within days of each other, one of which was to ask us if we'd be open to the possibility of adopting twins! ("Oh my gosh, yes . . . yes . . . YES!") And then, the heartbreaking silence would follow, letting us know by inference that the birth mom had selected a different family.

Alongside the discouragement, other haunting possibilities began to preoccupy us. Perhaps birth moms who carried a baby to term (rather than choosing abortion) were conservative in their mindset . . .? Maybe inviting such birth moms to consider a gay couple was already a stretch, and then we were adding all our additional uniqueness (freakiness, non-typicalness) into the mix—one prospective dad an artist who sells cosmetics, another who has hopped around the planet his whole life, living in more cities than the average human being even visits! Maybe the fact that we are an interracial couple was a problem . . .? Maybe it's the fact that we included Unitarian Universalism in our profile, a tradition most people know little to nothing about . . .? What if the birth moms thought that Unitarian Universalism is a cult, and then just move on to the next prospective family?

With deep pain in my heart, I approached my husband and asked him to consider whether we needed to revise our portfolio, and somehow try to come across as a more run-of-the-mill, "typical" family. Maybe what we needed to do was rewrite all our materials and emphasize all the ways in which we would be like some gay, interracial version of the *Brady Bunch*, and downplay, or not mention, the aspects of our lives that others might not relate to or understand . . .?

In the midst of this profoundly tortured handwringing, we received The Call. Yes, that one, the one that really mattered: a placement. "Come and meet your baby tomorrow morning. Can you do that?" (*"What? Twelve hours* from now? The baby is coming home with us . . . *tomorrow?"*) After a truly frenetic night of running to the local Walmart, minutes before the store closed at midnight, and anxiously buying way too much stuff from the baby aisle, the next day we got to meet our newborn child as well as the amazing birth mom who chose us over all other prospective families. As we talked to her, she shared with us how much she loved my husband's background in retail cosmetics; she had graduated from cosmetology school. She wanted her son to travel and see the world, just as I had. And while she did not personally know Unitarian Universalism, she thought that a child growing up in the midst of a loving, supportive spiritual community would be so beautiful. She saw who we are . . . and she chose us. With deep intention and careful deliberation, she truly chose *us*.

Our season of Advent was over, and the newborn babe arrived in our lives precisely because of our authenticity, not in spite of it. Just as Christmas Day yields to the New Year, our journey as parents had now begun.

Fertile Dreams

Vanessa Rush Southern

That you are having trouble conceiving doesn't hit you all at once. It comes month by month in increments. First, you laugh—you know, the whole irony about how hard you tried *not* to get pregnant all the years prior. If it continues, though, you cannot help but get a little nervous.

At first, you read more closely the chapters on fertility in the pregnancy books you bought. Then you buy whole books on conception. There are the dietary changes—no caffeine, more yams—then the acupuncture, the fertility yoga. Before too long you know more about the life cycle of eggs, sperm, and the whole human endocrine system than you ever dreamed you would. You know it is bad when you start to dream about fallopian tubes and drop words like *blastula* into dinner conversation with normal people. You are in the thick of it, the fog of it; stuck and mired in infertility.

In this place or time, things are rough. I remember the hopeful days when I would sense that perhaps I was feeling one or another of the physical signs of pregnancy; those same days turning into some of the worst of days, when it turned out I was wrong. Each month I didn't get pregnant was another occasion to grieve, a growing sense of failure at something that I wanted so badly and that no amount of hard work could achieve.

I was lucky, in the midst of my struggle with infertility, to find a therapist who knew firsthand about the experiences I was having. Nancy was beautiful and well put together and seemingly happy.

By the time I met her she had two adopted children, the mention of whom made her face light up. All of that mattered to me—it was hard evidence that I would (or could) come out of this chapter happy and whole, no matter where the journey took us. Plus, Nancy's experience and wisdom of having walked the journey of infertility herself meant she had so much to offer me. She regularly glued me back together and sent me back out into the world for the next round of living and "trying."

At one point in all this I came to her, distraught, because I realized that I had no dreams for my life or my work, and that scared me. It was fall and the time I do goal-setting professionally and personally. Previously I had always loved this process. I'd always been a person for whom possibilities or dreams for myself or my community came easily. But that year, that fall, nothing came to me. And it felt doubly cruel that here, in the midst of my struggle with infertility, when it felt like my body was betraying me, I had lost something else I had loved about myself and life.

After I told Nancy all this, she said quietly and without hesitation that I had it all wrong. "You have dreams, Vanessa," she said. "It's just that right now your dreams are about starting a family, and that is all your heart can hold."

She was right, of course. And in that moment I learned how our world can sometimes grow smaller and more intense for a while. How sometimes our dreams can be only for ourselves or some small part of our lives. How sometimes, at least for a time, that is all the heartbreak we can risk.

Thereafter, whenever people asked what they could do for me, I knew the answer. I needed them to wait with me. I needed them to be with me on the small island of hope that was all I dared lay claim to right then. I needed them just to keep me company there and pray.

Two Pink Lines

KATE LANDIS

When the two plus signs on the pregnancy test turned pink, I reached for the church phone directory. Well, first I reached for the phone book (this was before internet searches were common) and looked up abortion services, the very first listing in the heavy, yellow tome. I also had to weed out the Emergency Pregnancy Centers, those anti-abortion centers with ads that read "Pregnant? Need Help?" The only help there was a fundamentalist locking me up in a room and then reciting false statistics: abortion causes breast cancer, infertility, suicide, global warming, zombie apocalypse—none of which is true. No, thank you. I knew without the slightest doubt that I wanted to end this unexpected pregnancy. I just didn't know how a person went about choosing an abortion clinic.

Today I suppose I would check out Yelp reviews, but in conservative Cleveland, abortion was something people either didn't talk about or opposed. The Catholic diocese was next to the café where I worked, and nearly every day there were protestors outside with huge photos. The barbequed baby pictures, we called them—pictures of newborn babies covered in fake blood and barbeque sauce. They were supposed to be aborted fetuses but were laughably fake. My coworkers, none of whom were particularly religious or political, joked about the pictures—but as one woman said, "I think abortion is murder. But if my teenage daughter was raped, no one would know she was pregnant but me and Planned Parenthood." A good friend had a pregnancy scare and said that while pregnancy would be a disaster, she would never do "*that*, never kill a baby." I wasn't going to call her and ask what she had heard about the various clinics, much less ask my coworkers.

The phone book listed five available clinics: two Planned Parenthoods and three independents. The listings featured a butterfly, or a pencil outline of a thin woman's body, or clouds partially covering a sun. I wondered what each one was meant to represent, what vibe the clinics were attempting. I didn't know where to go, so I grabbed my church directory and flipped through the pages.

For around six months, I'd been going to a Unitarian Universalist church in my neighborhood. It was a small congregation meeting in an old Orthodox synagogue, a funny conflation of liberal hippies in jeans and activist t-shirts, same-sex couples, and trans folks walking into an old worship space where you could still see the demarcations between the curtained women's section of the synagogue and the men's. Unitarian Universalists believe that every faith tradition holds wisdom and that reason and science are as important as religious tradition. So my UU congregation had UU-Jews and UU-Buds (Unitarian Universalist Jews and Buddhists) as well as Christians, atheists, and a huge number of agnostics. What UU congregations share is not a common theology but a common purpose—living a meaningful and ethical life. Leaving the world better than we found it. We like to say "Deeds not Creeds": don't tell me what you believe; tell me how your beliefs move you to act in the world. What we do is more important than what we believe.

I had moved on the edges of the congregation for the past half a year, falling in love with them at a rate that scared me. I had been burned by church before. I didn't trust religion or religious people. Still, I was unable to resist the pull of this congregation. From the very first Sunday, I felt a force larger than me pushing me out my door and into the sanctuary. And from the start, this quirky assortment of church folk had embraced me, inviting me to sit with them during the service, putting mugs of hot coffee into my hands at social hour, interested in the few words I shared with them.

My goal had been to hover on the edges of church life indefinitely. I didn't want any more people knowing about my screwed-up life. But without realizing it, I found myself joining a local foods potluck group, teaching Sunday School to sweet middle school kids, even sometimes singing in the choir. People asked about my husband, Drew, and I made the excuses: that he was shy, that he worked odd hours. They got the hint and stopped asking about Drew but kept engaging me. Somehow, I had become a part of this big family. Suddenly, they were my favorite people in the world, and I was happier than I had been in years. I fit somewhere. I was wanted and deeply cared for.

And I was also pregnant, damn it. The timing was awful. My marriage was disintegrating; Drew was stoned constantly. I already resented having to feed, clothe, and care for him. We were barely getting by on my meager coffee shop salary. I still had panic attacks, and who knew if my depression would return?

I know that abortion stories are supposed to be full of logical reasons to end a pregnancy. Not enough money, an abusive partner, health risks. Motives listed so that a decision seems less selfish, seems like less of a choice and more of a tragedy. "I would have had that sweet little baby, but. . . ."

I had a handful of logical reasons not to want to be pregnant, but to be honest, I could have made parenthood work. I could have moved back in with my parents. Gone on low-income medical assistance. Called on aunts and uncles to babysit so I could work some job part-time. But I didn't want to be a mom. I never have. Even when playing house as a child, I wanted to be the big sister, never the mommy. I spent years caring for Drew and resenting it. I wasn't going to continue this pregnancy.

Women are taught to put other people's needs ahead of their own. That it is the natural order of things: for us to give all of our creativity and intelligence and energy, our whole selves, our whole lives, to caring for our children, spouses, and eventually aging parents. When I was little, I asked my teacher why some women didn't have children, and she said, "because they are selfish." It went against every notion of what a woman was supposed to be for me to want an abortion. I felt scalding shame over my lack of mothering instinct. Perhaps this was another facet of my mental illness? A chronic lack of a biological clock—was that in the DSM? From the moment a few days earlier when a wave of nausea made me think, *shit, am I pregnant?*, I knew I wasn't going to have a baby.

There was guilt, and plenty of shame, but no doubt. Parenthood was not in my future. I didn't have any doubts about ending the pregnancy, but I felt like I should. I felt like I should be sad, but I wasn't. I just felt relief that abortion was legal and accessible in my state. Did that make me a psychopath?

By that point, Drew and I were already in marriage counseling, although the odds looked bleaker and bleaker. I asked him if he felt guilty about my upcoming abortion. Raised Catholic, he had seen his share of barbequed baby pictures, heard sermons at mass about the sin of abortion. But he didn't feel any remorse. He said it was like I was having a root canal: it was a hassle that had to be dealt with so the condition wouldn't worsen. He didn't want to be a parent either and was relieved that, on this at least, we were in agreement. Did that make me not crazy? Or just both of us crazy?

All around us, friends and family acted like abortion was a necessary evil. Abortion was for worst-case-scenario pregnancies. But we just didn't want to have a baby. Was that a good enough reason?

Ohio's restrictive abortion laws meant I needed to hurry up and find a clinic, make an appointment, and have the procedure. I didn't know how long I had been pregnant, but after the first trimester I wouldn't be allowed to terminate my pregnancy in Ohio and would have to find the money to travel to a more woman-friendly state for the procedure. I didn't get paid time off work and wasn't sure how I was going to afford an abortion here, much less in another state. So I needed an appointment fast.

I vaguely remembered a woman at church, Martha, talking about working at an abortion clinic: about a bomb threat that had shut them down for a few hours, about the panic of patients who were terrified that the threat would bring reporters. That they might be on the news, spotted at an abortion clinic. How depressing was it that women were petrified that they would be caught having a legal medical procedure? The stigma around pregnancy termination meant that women were more worried about being seen at the clinic than about the alleged bomb.

I didn't know Martha, but we shared a church and a church family I had unwittingly fallen in love with. We were bound together by that quirky community in that old synagogue. I didn't have to know her to know that she cared about me. However, when she picked up the phone, I found myself suddenly tongue-tied. What if Martha said I didn't deserve an abortion? What if she said that my reasons weren't good enough? Maybe there was a test to pass, a test to determine if I really deserved an abortion. Would I need to prove my dire circumstances? I babbled into the phone, talking around my question, telling her I was thinking of what she had said at church about being a nurse. She asked if I was thinking of going into nursing, and I replied "No. . . ."

After a few moments of awkward silence, she said, "Oh, do you need an abortion, honey?" I said, "Yes, I need a recommendation—who has the best abortions in town?" I'm not sure what I meant by "the best," but Mary laughed and said they were all pretty good, equally safe, the same cost—but that there was a considerable shortage of abortion providers in the area and so clinics were booked up weeks in advance, if not months. She understood my worry about entering my second trimester and said she would find a time to squeeze me in at her clinic to at least see how far along I was.

A few days later, I was at the clinic getting an ultrasound. I was five weeks pregnant, an embryo smaller than a millimeter barely visible on the monitor. A tiny fleck of white on the black screen. I was tremendously relieved that I could have an abortion in my home state. It would have been nearly impossible for me to find the funds to go out of state for the procedure, and I would certainly have lost my job for missing so many days of work. But I was within the first trimester window. Exhausted from vomiting multiple times a day, charley horses, and all food tasting like metal, I scheduled my abortion for just two days later.

Abortion Day arrived humid and sunny. I was nervous; I had never had surgery or anesthesia. The nurse led me to a waiting room where, sitting in my thin hospital gown, I flipped through magazines next to another silent woman. I began to panic about the procedure—would it be painful? What if there were complications and I ended up in the hospital? Who would I have to tell then? As disastrous scenarios sped through my mind, the woman next to me began to cry.

Her hands were clasped tightly in front of her, her curly hair obscuring my view of her face. She began to sort of moan and rock back in forth. I asked her if she was okay, and she nodded yes, but her cries got louder.

"I can't believe I'm doing this. This is so messed up."

"Is someone making you? You don't have to—it's up to you."

She laughed bitterly. "Up to me. Great. Because I've done such a great job with my life so far. I have two kids. They're at school; I have to get this done with before they get out of school. I called in sick. I better not get fired."

She caught her breath, looking at me defensively. "I have to do this for my kids. I can barely feed them, keep them housed. I don't know how I'm going to buy their school supplies. This isn't a choice. I can't have a baby. We'd be on the street."

I said I was sorry, and she cried a while longer. Then, catching her breath, she said, "The thing is, I know God won't forgive me. It's not a forgivable sin. There are some rules you don't break. So I'll go to Hell. I'll go to Hell for this, ripping this baby out of me. Killing it. But I have to do it. I can't put my kids on the street."

I don't know what I replied. Her despair broke my heart. She truly believed that she was going to Hell for having an abortion, but she would choose Hell over hurting her kids. It was beautiful and terrible, this motherly sacrifice. I opened my mouth to comfort her. I wanted to talk about the God I believe in, who created abortion providers because motherhood is a sacred covenant, an agreement that not every pregnant person is in a position to make. That motherhood is a choice, and pregnancy is a question: will you continue toward parenthood? It was wonderful that she wanted to protect her two children from poverty by saying no to this pregnancy. But before I formed the words, the nurse called her into the operating room. I never saw her again.

I prayed desperately for her in the operating room, still doubting her decision. I prayed for me and for all the women and girls who have to make decisions about their bodies under enormous social and religious pressure. I prayed that we be able to hear the wisdom of our own hearts over the screaming demands of our culture that we sacrifice our own lives to care for other people. That we hear our own wisdom over the tyranny of patriarchal religions, faiths that deny the whole personhood of women, that limit their growth and freedom. In the waiting room, I was filled with gratitude for the women who worked around me in the clinic, the nurses and aides, administrators and doctors, accountants and custodians who risked social stigma and bodily harm to come to work every day so that I could be free of forced pregnancy. Our creator has gifted them with enormous bravery and graciousness.

Soon it was my turn for the operating room. I thanked God one last time for this freedom to choose or not choose motherhood and then walked inside. I laid down on the table and admitted to the nurse that I was quite nervous. She took my hand and spoke in soft, comforting tones about exactly how the operation would proceed. The doctor told me my anesthesia options, and I chose to have a local numbing agent rather than sleeping through the procedure. Sleep sounded relaxing but cost an extra $200. Soon the doctor fed a thin tube up inside my uterus. There was a loud, mechanical hum, and I felt a strong pinch in my low stomach and then cramps no worse than those during my menstrual cycle. Then the tube was coming out and the doctor said, "You are no longer pregnant!" in a celebratory way. I started to cry from relief and thanked them both profusely, and we all hugged. I said, "Thank you, thank you, thank you" to God, and then I was off to the recovery room to drink juice and eat cookies in a lounge chair.

I bled for a month afterward, every day like the heaviest day of my period. I felt 10 percent annoyed by it and 90 percent relieved that

I had access to a safe, sanitary abortion. I didn't feel like I could talk to many of my friends about this life-changing procedure. I was still tender-hearted from losing my community in college when I was depressed. What if I told my friends and they rejected me? What if they said my reasons for having an abortion were not good enough?

This was the most consequential decision I had ever made, and I felt more in control of my own future than ever before. I had married due to love, sure, but also family pressure. I chose my college based on financial aid. Drew and I moved to Cleveland because he wanted to be close to his brothers. This was the first choice I had made independently, by myself and for myself alone. I felt that a rite of passage had occurred. I had come to a fork in the road and chosen a definite direction. I was proud.

I turned to my church community to celebrate. I brought Martha a homemade pie the next Sunday morning at church. When people asked why, I told some of them, the ones I trusted the most: Martha had helped me get an abortion. They hugged me. Women shared their own abortion stories and their own feelings of deep relief. We talked about God and gratitude for our freedom to choose motherhood, or not.

It is powerful to belong to a faith community that sees women as whole, holy people. We are capable of making decisions about parenthood, about pregnancy, about our future. Too many faiths seek to take away the God-given independence that strengthens women. Too many churches say that women aren't moral enough to control their own fertility, that we need laws and limits to keep us from making real choices. Motherhood is a holy covenant, not to be interfered with by men or legislation.

God didn't create women just to raise children, just to be helpmates, to serve other people. We are imbued with our own creative power. We make our own destinies. Motherhood wasn't what I wanted. I am not ashamed.

A few weeks after my abortion, when my bleeding was beginning to lessen, I had a dream. In it, I was sitting on the back steps in my parents' yard, crying, my hands covering my face. I felt a small hand shaking my shoulder and through my fingers saw a little girl, four or five, leaning in to look at me. "Mommy, mommy," she said. "It's okay, Mommy, I'm fine. I'm fine!" And then that little spirit ran away from me to spin in circles in the yard, laughing and looking at the sky.

A Helicopter Pilot

CHERYL M. WALKER

As a woman, I often get asked the question "Do you have any children?" The people asking are never my friends, because my friends already know the answer. Many times the questioner is a complete stranger who feels they have the right to ask such a personal question. I'm sure they think it's just small talk, but I find the question rather rude. My answer is "No, I do not." This is usually followed by their second question: "Did you ever want to have children?"

This is a terrible question for many reasons. Maybe I did want to have children but was unable to have them. Then the question would make me relive the pain of not being able to be a parent. Or perhaps I did have a child that died, and the question would make me relive the unimaginable, the loss of a child. Even if these are not the reasons I answered "no" to the first question, underlying the second question is an assumption that I *should* have wanted to have children. After all, no one asks someone they barely know, "Did you want to be a helicopter pilot?" because only under very rare circumstances would we assume someone would have wanted to be a helicopter pilot—maybe they are wearing a t-shirt that says "I love helicopters." For the record, I never wanted to have children; I may have wanted to be a helicopter pilot.

When I tell people I never wanted to have children, they make an awful lot of assumptions about why. The simple truth is I just never wanted to have children, so I didn't. I didn't choose *not* to have children, I just didn't choose *to* have children. As a lesbian woman

I found it easy not to have children, which is not to say that I didn't want children because I am a lesbian. I know plenty of lesbian moms, some of whom gave birth to children and some of whom adopted children. I'm just not one of them.

People assume that I don't like children, and that is why I never had them. I actually love children. There are children in my life and I enjoy them, except when they're three; three-year-olds are amoral beings who lie, cheat, and steal. Luckily they eventually turn four, after which I learn to like them again. Some of the greatest joys in my life have been attending the births of my nieces and nephews, and even the birth of my niece's child. I love being called "Auntie" and "Grantie."

People assume I am selfish for not having children. And there may be a modicum of truth to that; it's what I wanted. I wanted a life without rearing children. But there's another truth: choosing to have a child is also an act of selfishness. There are no unselfish reasons for having a child, no matter why you wanted one. We are all selfish in our own ways.

People assume that because I don't have children I don't have family obligations, and therefore have more time and money. But it is often those of us without children who bear a larger responsibility for aging parents. Siblings will often look to us to take care of parents because we don't have children who need our attention. I took care of my aging parents and I was glad to do so because I could, but not everyone can. In some families it is the siblings with children who have more resources because they have more income earners. Until recently, as a society, we didn't give family leave to people except to take care of children. I could have used some leave time when my parents were aging and needed more of my time. Instead I had to use up all of the vacation and personal time I had. I don't resent taking care of my parents; I do resent the fact that our society afforded me no support.

There are so many assumptions people make about those of us who do not have children. Almost all of them are false. While the overwhelming number of adult women have children, there is nothing wrong with those of us who chose not to have them. Having a child is not the ultimate purpose of being a woman. It could be to pilot a helicopter.

Letter to Lyla

Marlin Lavanhar

It is Thanksgiving 2008, three weeks before you are expected to be born. My heart is overflowing with love and joy knowing that I will meet you soon. It is as if my heart is going to burst from a love too big to contain.

I wanted to write to tell you when I first felt your presence in my life and when I first felt the touch of your spirit. It was a spring evening in Tulsa with a crystal-clear sky and a gentle, warm breeze that was only detectable if one was really paying attention. It was May 8 of this year and I was sitting with my good friend Pat in his backyard. He had suggested we visit to talk about my feelings about adoption. Your mom and I were trying to decide if we were going to adopt. She was ready before I was, so Pat wanted a chance to help me explore my feelings. After about two hours of wonderful discussion about life and children and marriage and God, Pat took my hand into his much larger hand as we sat side by side. We peered up together through the gentle rustling leaves of a tall tree. We were beneath a huge canopy of stars and a radiant, waxing crescent moon. It was as if we were looking out into the whole of the universe. Pat said, "This is an important decision. There's a soul out there somewhere for whom your decision really matters." As those words penetrated my heart, they also seemed to radiate out to the edges of creation. At that moment I felt the presence of your soul for the first time. It was as real a feeling as the pull of gravity holding me to the earth. It was unmistakable.

After a long silence, filled with the presence of your essence, we prayed that I would do my part to make sure that I did right by your soul. What that meant was that if it were not right for me to adopt, then I should not adopt. That decision mattered too. But in that sacred silence, I felt my heart say "Yes" to you. I felt your warmth and power to the core of my being. I had no idea who you were, but I knew you were out there and that I needed to do my work to become ready for you. That night, you were conceived spiritually as my daughter. It is a connection as deep as, and deeper than, a mere biological one. I claimed you that night, not as my property, but as one who has been entrusted to me, to care for and to help become whom God has intended you to become. Today I stand open and committed to do whatever I can to father you to become all that you are meant to be.

A Friendly's Ice Cream Baby

David O. Rankin

It was a long journey on a cold winter day. Our destination was Framingham, Massachusetts. Even our wedding, nine years before, had been easier on our nerves!

This shopping mall was one of those brick and plastic affairs with a slick New England façade and two banks for every store . . .

We parked the car somewhere on the twenty acres of cement and walked to the Friendly's ice cream store. Inside, we were pushed to a booth in the rear.

A listless waitress tried to memorize our order . . . The [restaurant] was crowded at noon. People were munching hamburgers, slurping coffee, and drowning in ice cream. They were far too busy to witness a miracle!

When the social worker arrived, she held a large screaming bundle in her arms. The customers muttered and groaned. "Get the baby out!" they seemed to say.

Little did they know I had just heard my daughter.

Little did they know I had just adopted a child.

Little did they know I had just seen the face of God.

I wonder: did the cries of the child in Bethlehem disturb the revelers at the inn?

To Life Ordained

JANE RZEPKA

It was almost fifty years ago that I first left my new baby, Adam, in someone else's hands for the evening. The memory is strong—the concern, the aching, the missing, pure and simple. Not a part of me wanted to leave that baby. But I did. I was being ordained.

Ministers often write about what a special day their ordination was. They quote wise words that have held them in such good stead and recall the personal and religious gravity they felt during the service. I want to do that too. But all I remember is missing my baby.

To life ordained, to be sure. I know that all parents feel The Tug Writ Large, the tug between our kids and whatever else life asks of us. Maybe you're in the midst of your Big Presentation and the daycare center calls. Or you have to ask your boss for an unscheduled break because your teenager is in tears, their most recent love having ghosted them. Or your mother, two hours away, has a stroke as you head out the door for the school play. For ministers, it's something like getting the call that a parishioner has died just as your child's birthday party begins. Most of us muddle through. Muddle. Muddle again. And again, trying to balance it all.

I love the ministry and I loved being ordained into it. But my ordination was different: I learned that night about the power of caring, the wrench of separation, the ambiguity of responsibility, and the joy of reunion.

Now and then a wise word or two comes back to me from that long-ago ceremony, and the gravity too. But ministry would never completely occupy center stage—I knew that now. Joined in the spotlight was my newborn son, wrinkled and pink, full of promise.

Setting a Course for Love

Peggy Clarke

In 1945, my grandmother, Dorothy, had a very young daughter (my mother) and was married to my grandfather, who we now understand had an undiagnosed case of bipolar disorder. Glass broken in anger, blood on the living room floor, and howling threats were part of life in their one-bedroom apartment. Young women with little children in the 1940s were sometimes faced with difficult marriages, but divorce was a radical and rarely considered option. My grandmother didn't know anyone who had ever left their husband, and it was clear in her Jewish, Eastern European neighborhood on the Lower East Side of Manhattan that this was not something one did.

Grandmother, however, wasn't generally beholden to rules and she was pretty desperate. After a particularly frightening night, she took her three-year-old daughter and went to her parents' house, seeking their support were she to divorce. Less an announcement and more a request, this was going to be a painful and complicated conversation. She risked being shunned by her family, left with the options of returning to her husband or raising her daughter entirely alone in a cold water flat.

Grandma Dorothy was particularly afraid of speaking with her father. She was the oldest of four and the family needed her to be financially independent; there was no extra money or an extra room for an adult child to come home, let alone one with a toddler in tow. Working women in the 1940s had a difficult time supporting themselves and the term "single mother" hadn't even been coined yet.

Dorothy left her daughter with her own mother in the kitchen and went to talk with her father alone. "Papa," she said, "I have to leave Joe. I don't think we're safe there. I'm sorry, but I can't go back, and I don't know what to do or where to go."

My great-grandfather stayed silent for some time. He sat in his chair, looking sad while Dorothy waited. In the still, quiet living room while she was waiting, she knew these could be the last few moments she'd be welcome in her parents' home, and as anxious as she was to hear his response, she was less eager about what could happen next. She wouldn't have been the first woman in her neighborhood who tried to end her marriage only to be sent back to an abusive husband under threat of being disowned.

Finally my great-grandfather, her father, stood up and walked over to her. He put his arms around her and said, "We are your family. You are always safe here. We'll figure it out together."

That was it. This has been our sacred story ever since: the moment in our history when my great-grandparents embodied love, creating our family culture for generations. My parents rehearsed this lesson every time one of their kids was struggling or was in crisis. Divorce, unemployment, illness, the message has continued through the years. "You're always safe here. We'll figure it out together."

View from the
Dining Room Table

SARAH LENZI

Some years ago, my father and I sat at the dining room table; my parents and I share an apartment. We were watching my three children in the living room. They were playing. Shouting. Being the six- and three- and three-year-olds they were. Without turning to look at me, my father said, his voice thick with tears, "I wish I would be around to see who they are when they grow up."

My father wasn't dying. He's had both hips replaced in the last year, and he has survived the pandemic in a city hit incredibly hard at the outset. While not exactly hale, he turns out to be hearty. I assume it is his northern Italian, alpine ancestry. But my father suffers, as I do, from a certain kind of melancholia, if you'll pardon the use of such an old-fashioned term. In that moment at our shared, multigenerational dining room table, he vulnerably spoke to a fear that grips me often and to an understanding that I live with always: the fear that I will be separated from my children before my work raising them to adulthood is done, and the understanding that, inevitably, we will all lose each other.

When I was twenty-eight, I decided to spend one year trying to meet a man I wanted to marry and spend my life with; perhaps more to the point, a man who wanted that with me. It didn't happen. I determined to do what for some time I had thought would be my fate (self-fulfilling prophecy, yes, maybe): have children on my own by using a sperm donor. A decision such as this, though shared by a surprising number of folks from all walks of life and sexual orientations, still remains a somewhat rare one. And oh, the stories I could tell! Of peers who likened my choice to eugenics; of men who react against their implied obsolescence when they hear my story; of the day at another dining room table when I wept, trying to convince my father that I didn't need to wait any longer in hopes of meeting a man who wanted me; of those who still wonder why I didn't adopt; of the number of times I have been called brave or courageous. There are so many stories. And I don't know about brave; more often than not I wonder if I was selfish. But ultimately, I reached the decision because, more than anything in life, I knew that I was called to motherhood. More than my studies, my ministry, more than anything else, from the time I was small, I wanted children. I wanted to know what it felt like to create life, to bring it forth, to raise children into this world.

It took five tries to get pregnant the first time. My oldest child was born late in the year I turned thirty. In spite of my lifelong longing, I didn't have that magical moment movies and television say we should, that moment of instantly loving this tiny red-faced being. My first baby instantly had my fierce protective instinct and my determination to keep alive this thing I had created, but my love, the deep kind we feel for others whom we truly know and who know us, that came for me in time. It came through exhaustion and middle-of-the-night feedings and endless snuggles and wailing cries (from both of us). I had always known that I wanted my child to have a sibling; when I was young I wanted six kids! Undertaking this alone, I felt even more strongly that my child would need another who would understand what it was to be born to just me. I had my twins shortly after I turned thirty-four. I learned then a whole new world of tiredness and frustration and determination.

Life is full. Full of noise and commotion and worry.

Life is hard. We get on each others' nerves. The compromises of parenting sometimes make me want to run away and paint (poorly) the landscape of Italy in the late-afternoon Tuscan sun; that urge has come often to this introvert living through a global pandemic in the constant company of five other folks in a NYC apartment. What I would give for an afternoon of true unfettered solitude!

Life is often lonely. Parenting without a partner eases a lot—I need not consult another, I just get to decide. There are no disappointed hopes because I imagined my partner would do this or help that way and they didn't. But it also hurts a lot—there is no sharing the burden or the blame. As helpful as grandparents are, and they are, the decisions are mine alone. There is a loneliness to single parenting that I suspect only other single parents can comprehend.

And life brings abundant questions. Questions from them about who their "dad" is. Questions from others about why they only have one mom and why their grandparents live with us. Questions from my own heart about who they will become and the phases they will move through as they navigate the circumstances of their birth, so different from that of other children.

No practice, no spiritual preaching, no wisdom tradition, no service to a congregation, nothing in life has taught me more about dwelling in the questions, the uncertainty, and the lack of control than parenting. Nothing has taught me more about my capacity to love, more about my capacity to fear, and more about my own power than this work of motherhood. Until children, my life was largely defined by measurable successes: good grades received, applications to schools accepted, desirable jobs gotten, good friends made and kept, dreams achieved. But children? They are not measurable, and no amount of preparedness actually prepares us for parenting. The great lie of my 1980s girl-baby life, that control is possible and that if we work hard enough we can achieve anything and have it all, was exposed in no uncertain terms when my children were infants and together we faced projectile vomit and concussion watches and a three-day hospital stay the first Christmas the twins were alive. As they have grown the lie has been again and again disproved. My children ask questions I don't expect, about life and sex and big emotions and who they are. They behave in unpredictable ways. And in spite of having nearly ten years of parenting under my belt, I still get frustrated and irritable and done when I wish I had more to give. I expect that no matter how many more years I am blessedly given with my children, there will be still be unanswered questions from all of us, I will be caught off guard, I will wish that my love and care and attention alone could keep them safe and whole and well, and I will recognize that my love and my fear belong together as I try to teach my children that though life can be scary, it is beautiful and precious and measured not by successes we can count on our fingers but by the very fear and love we are willing to let live in our open hearts, that break and mend and stretch again and again.

When I look at my children, some days I am overcome. Tears arise unbidden as I wonder who they will be. A fervent prayer erupts from my heart, crying out to the divine I know, pleading that I may be lucky enough to be around to know these children as grownups, as partners and parents if they choose those paths. My prayer is that I may know them for as long as possible, through all their seasons of chaos and questions.

I don't know what the future will bring into my life or theirs. But every day I can sit at the dining room table and watch them be themselves, even when it is heartbreaking and hard and I am angry or ornery and so are they, is one more day of fulfilling the deepest calling of my own heart. And I am grateful.

You Have No Idea

Lindasusan V. Ulrich

Within the first few minutes after we met—he one week old, me in my forties—he peed on me. I knew this was something baby boys do, and when we said yes to fostering him, I wasn't sure how I'd handle it. "Well," I thought, "I guess we got that out of the way."

He met all of his milestones right on time: rolling over, standing, walking, talking. Around age three, though, something seemed amiss. Other parents shared stories of meltdowns and aggression by their three-year-olds, but they didn't seem to have the same haunted look that lived in our eyes. They also didn't have kids with early trauma. We started looking for a child psychologist. Many more professionals would follow.

He charmed people everywhere he went. Not intentionally— he just exuded charisma. Adults in the grocery store would spontaneously give him a dollar, just because. With his curly brown hair and hazel eyes, he was beautiful as well. One photo I snapped at a playground looked like it came straight from an OshKosh B'Gosh ad campaign. I spent serious thought on how to make sure he'd only use his charm for good, not ill.

At some point, starting medication became the obvious choice. Dear friends whose daughter also has ADHD shared her doctor's analogy: the meds help them focus, just like glasses help your eyes focus. What a difference! We soared on that hopeful cloud for a while . . . and then the aggression came back. His doctor would up the medication, and again we'd see improvement. We held off each increase as long as possible, wanting to delay the day when he'd max out on the dosage.

During our rides to preschool, he wanted me to make up stories while we drove, mainly based on Fireman Sam. Over time, we concocted a world that brought superheroes and supervillains to Pontypandy, with story arcs that would carry on for weeks. He came up with some truly innovative twists that I never would have thought of myself. I delighted in his joyous creativity.

Flipping desks. Ripping down posters in the classroom. Throwing things at other students. Doing restorative circles with his classmates. Running out of the building and around the block. Kindergarten brought many phone calls and multiple suspensions. Given how often we were getting hit at home, none of this came as a surprise.

You'd be hard-pressed to find a kid more generous than ours. For example, as a three-year-old, he'd offer to share his donut with other kids. Recently, we circled the block two extra times when we were already late for an appointment because he wanted to give his bag of candy to the person who'd asked us for food at a red light.

How is the child who lugs his giant unicorn stuffies outside to show to his new friends the same one who calls us bitches and throws shoes at our heads? I don't know how many times I've gone to the emergency room or urgent care to get injuries looked at. I've also lost track of how many times I didn't even bother.

After the first dozen concussions, what are they going to tell me that I haven't heard before?

He is genuinely hilarious. Not just oh-isn't-that-cute funny, but spontaneous-belly-laugh funny. He's also whip-smart, excellent at reading and building. He loves making art. I'm hoping his love of music will inspire him to join the youth choir at the congregation I serve.

"I'm sorry, Mama! I'm sorry." He comes to comfort me as I'm wracked with sobs yet again. For better and worse, he also knows something is amiss.

Living with a child who hurts you isn't like having an abusive partner: you can't break up with your child.

At what point is unconditional love not enough?
How do you maintain a neutral, non-anxious presence
when you're getting beaten up?
When do the expected sacrifices of parenthood
become the unsought martyrdom of body, mind, emotion, and soul?
How do you live with the tender heartbreak
of your beloved young one causing you so much pain and fear?

For those of us for whom
parenting is a primary spiritual practice,
there are no easy answers
when parenting
breaks your spirit
every
single
day.

There's only
watching
hoping
trying
loving
and
holding on
for dear life.

Naming and Claiming

HEATHER CONCANNON

For Micah.

We started with "Auntie."

You are eighteen hours old when I first meet you.
It doesn't stick.

Next we tried "housemate,"
though people always think I mean an adult
as I walk around with you strapped to my chest
kissing the soft spot on your head.

In January my dad dies. You, nine months old and crawling,
come to his wake
with your Papa.
I hold you through most of it
because I can't stand to make small talk
with all those people.

You and I start to spend a full day together,
once a week.

Your parents and I and three other adults
buy a large house
and we all move in together.

When you start talking, it's "Hiya,"
which you repeat at our prompting
singsong-y,
so charming and cute.
The first name you use for me.

Mama and I
are both pretty sure we are there for your first steps.
I say the bedroom,
Mama says the pediatrician's office.
Papa was there for both
but I think he has lost track of the timeline,
or perhaps just doesn't want to upset anyone.

Out in the world sometimes
people ask me how old my baby is.
"Fourteen months," I say, dodging.

I never confirm that you are mine,
but I won't say you are not mine, either.
I never want you to think I don't claim you.

And I wonder:
what does it mean to belong to another person,
anyway?

I permanently install a car seat
and you permanently install a layer of cheerios and raisins
in my car.

Around two, I get "go 'way!" shouted at me
more often than not,
with all the attendant rudeness of a securely attached toddler.

Sometimes I feel like *that* might as well be my name.

I tell you "I love you"
for the five thousandth time
and you look right at me,
and for the first time you respond with
"I love *you!*"

We are camping.
You and I are hanging out in my small tent
to keep you away from the bugs.

Today is my birthday.

I am delighted.

I find a caterpillar
and you and I spend a whole summer
raising monarchs together.

You and Mama and I
go to Star Island together,
for a week.
Just the three of us.

Sometimes we spend several weeks apart
when one of us is traveling.

We don't do family vacations together,
mostly.

For that matter, I also don't do
pediatrician's appointments
middle of the night wakeups
bed-wettings
daycare decisions
vomiting
money
or mornings.

I do do diaper changes,
potty training,
daycare pickups,
Buy Nothing posts,
imagining you as a teenager,
meals,
snacks,
sharing germs,
adventures,
errands,
pee in my car,
naps together,
tantrums,
baths,
and bedtimes.

Together,
you and I make cookies and art projects,
fairy houses,
cards that we mail to people,

dinner,
messes,
protest signs,
video calls,
negotiations,
music,
silly games,
and more.

You exhaust me.
Sometimes I count the minutes
until I hand you off to Mama and Papa at the end of our day,
but I always want more time with you.

I make your Halloween costume.
A monarch butterfly
inside a silk green chrysalis.

You are very popular on my Instagram.

I wonder who people think you are to me.

At some point, you switch from "Hiya" to "Heder."

I am a little sad,
"Hiya" was so sweet,
but now you stretch out the R
so much it sounds like a W
and that makes me melt.

We are cooking together when you figure out
counting.

How each number
means one specific discrete object.
I hand you the bouillon cubes
and show you how to count them, slowly, one by one, for the
fourth time.
Dinner is a few minutes late
but the look of sudden comprehension on your face
is worth every second.

I give you your first haircut.

I tell my mom
I'm worried that if I have my own kid
I won't love them
as much as I love you.

She laughs at me and reassures me that she loves my younger
sister.

You are describing a scenario in your mind
that involves you getting hurt.
I ask you who would help you
and you say "well, my grown-ups would . . ."
and I ask you who you mean,
and you say, as though it's obvious:
"Mama, Papa, and Heder!"

I make your Halloween costume again.
This year, a fierce dragon.
I spend way more money on a homemade costume

than I would just buying it.

But I love doing a project
for you.

I repainted the sturdy bed my dad built for me
when I was five
and now you sleep in it
every night.

You call my cats "our cats,"
which I didn't teach you to do.
And you call our household "our family,"
which I did.

I fill your bookshelf with all the leftist kids' books I've been
curating over the years
for church.
I've brought them home during the pandemic,
ostensibly to read to the church kids on Zoom,
but mostly
I just read them to you.

We make up stories.
About Peter Rabbit and Baby Dragon
and fairies.
Fairies—who, I tell you,
love anything that brings
more kindness,
and fairness,

and beauty
into the world.

We build a fairy house in our backyard
a few weeks after telling you about a man named George
whose skin was black
and who was killed by a police officer in Minneapolis.
We took you to a protest
and told you how sad and angry all the people there are
about a terrible thing we call racism.

And in the backyard you tell me
that the fairies, who love kindness and fairness and beauty,
need a Black Lives Matter sign for their house
so we make a tiny sign
out of birch bark and sticks.

I notice and celebrate your tiny victories:
when you take a deep breath and don't hit anyone
even though you are so mad.
When you figure out how to get the socks off your little feet
without help,
when you finally start cooperating with toothbrushing,
when you recognize a new letter.

Mama, Papa, and I all take you
to the preschool orientation,
for you to meet your teachers.
It's on the playground.
Everyone is wearing masks.

Your grown-ups

are talking to the preschool director about pickup procedures.
You are shy at first around your new classmates.
Your new teacher skillfully tries to engage you,
as all three of us watch
out of the corners of our eyes.

Soon you are chatty,
and we overhear you saying to your peers
and teachers
gesturing toward us,
with a three-year-old's confidence
that your own little world is the norm:

"I gots a Mama, a Papa, and a Heder!"

These days,
I don't mind
if the rest of the world never understands who we are to each
other.
I'm not sure I understand myself, all the time.
I am at peace with it.

Because when I look at you,
I just feel gratitude,
pride and awe
and worry and curiosity
and tenderness and love—

so much love—

knowing
I am
your Heather.

Andre

RICHARD DAVIS-LOWELL

A parental tug

Merry Christmas, Andre:

"Did you try to call me this morning? I've got two missed calls from you."... "I'm surprised that you're still in bed—just waking up, I see."... "Oh, those calls were from yesterday? Okay."... "I woke you up?"... "No? Are you sure?"... "Well—Merry Christmas!"

Funny how we're tied together, after all these years. I notice things, especially in extreme close up . . . as on a cellphone video call.

"Andre, I'm really enjoying looking up your nose. Could you move the camera, please?"... "Here . . . let me show you what I see!" Half an eye in the corner of the screen, a camera shot right up the nostril. "This is what I see!" We laugh. "You know . . . what's the use of a video call if we can't see each other?"

"Are you sure you were up?" I ask. "You're still in bed." He yawns. Note to self . . . make sure he keeps that dental appointment. Why does nag mode always kick in? *Don't nag, just let it be,* I think.

There it is again, that feeling that says, "I want the best for you." But another voice assures me that right here, right now, this is enough . . . for him and for me. "Good morning, Mr. A!" Both cameras slightly askew.

In the little self-image on my phone, I see my own bags and lines, my own hair sticking up. "Good morning, Andre. Merry Christmas . . . are you okay?" "Yeah . . ." comes the reply . . . and another yawn. "How's Uncle?" "Bill's right here next to me . . . Say hello," I say. "Hey, Uncle Bill," he calls out. "Merry Christmas!" We're just here on Christmas morning . . . at 6:30 a.m. Andre's gift to me. "Are you going to make some of your best biscuits?" he asks.

Looking back

How many Christmases has it been? Y2K seems like a lifetime ago. You were fifteen and now you're thirty-five, and I was, well, younger. How can you be that old? How can I? But here we are. We are what we are, and I remember how it started.

An email from HR. "Interested in giving back?" it asked. "Big Brothers, Big Sisters is hosting an informational meeting next Tuesday . . . click here." How many other clicks have proven so consequential? Maybe one or two . . . but for this one, I'm forever grateful.

I remember an orientation, followed by a questionnaire and an essay, followed by a visit to a Dickensian San Francisco police station. Fingerprints taken on ancient equipment . . . rolled ink and paper . . . really? Waiting until the prints clear, a background check, references, then interviews, in person and at home.

Sitting on the couch with Bill in our living room, I think, *Is this what adoptive parents go through?* Solid, clear answers, honesty . . . steering the conversation . . . never forgetting we are being vetted . . . a strange sort of "competition," a competition to influence a life.

Later, as I'm sitting down with my advisor, she says, "Richard, I think I have someone special for you. Would you consider someone with special needs?" *Special needs?* I think. *What does that mean . . .*

like dietary restrictions, problems in school? I am perplexed. "No," she explains. "Special needs means developmental disability. Would you consider mentoring someone with developmental disabilities?"

My mind flashed. *What a question! Who would say "no way" to that?* I thought, and *Why even ask a question like that?*

I thought harder. After all, I hadn't specified who I wanted to mentor (can you even do that?), only that I wanted to be a mentor. "Well, you said you thought we'd be a good match . . . so then no, I don't mind, I don't mind at all," I said.

What I remember more clearly is pulling up to a high school's portable classroom on a Saturday morning and finding my way to the agreed-upon room. Inside, a young, skinny kid of about fifteen or so, looking down at his feet, with his mother and grandmother beside him . . . and my advisor, all there for an introductory meeting.

A flash thought. *Dear god . . . gays and young men! What do I remember about that supposed toxic brew? What will they think! What am I thinking?* Then, as if on cue, my advisor asks, "Andre, do you mind that Richard is gay?" Right in front of his mother and grandmother. "Nah . . . I don't care," comes the reply. His first gift to me.

And to his mother and grandmother: "Rose and Marie, do you mind that Richard is gay?" "No . . . only that he's a good person." Another gift.

So we were matched. I agreed to see Andre at least four times a month for a year. Check-ins with the agency every other week, with ongoing support as needed.

I did my best to be the "ideal" mentor. I dug out all the weekend suggestions from the newspaper and planned our outings to a "T" . . . but planning something "new and different" every week got to be overwhelming. After all, how many times can you go to a park, out on a fishing boat, or to a nursery?

"Andre," I said, "I'm running out of things for us to do . . . so you're just going to have to come with me on a Costco run." "I love Costco!" he said. It wasn't what we did that was important . . . it was that we did something together, another gift. So trips to the dry cleaner, grocery store, hardware store, pet store, and everything else were on.

No matter how bad my day had been or how tired I was, after spending a few minutes with Andre, hearing about his day and his challenges, I forgot about mine. More gifts . . . and the years rolled on, challenges coming and going.

One day I share, "You know, Andre, we're 'family of choice.' You can't choose your biological family, but each of us can create a family of choice." He thinks, then echoes, "That's what we are, Brother Richard: family of choice."

So many adventures . . . so many stories. "You say your dad's in jail again? That doesn't make sense . . . I'm so sorry, Andre." . . . "It's hard to explain . . . he's a grown man. But I don't understand why he doesn't want to see me," Andre shares. Neither of us understands.

It's the tough times that make the good times so much sweeter . . . and both follow. I've gone places I'd never dreamed I'd have to go. "Brother Richard, can you help me meet girls?" Gulp! Is this really a part of the script? I need some help here! "Let's talk to Bill!" I offer. Depression, hospitals, vacations, divorces, dad dying, dogs dying, life does its best, and still the gifts keep coming.

"Brother Richard . . . Merry Christmas . . . thanks for the Roku. And thank Uncle for the new phone." "You're welcome, Andre." "Yeah, I love you guys . . . I wish I could see you guys." "No, Andre, remember COVID." "Yeah … I know, but it gets to me." "Us too, but we have video right now … and we have each other. Remember that, right now … and we're family, family of choice."

Eyes Like Mine

MARCIA STANARD

It's the Facebook Memories that get me. Mika saying, "When I think about family, I picture the six of us gathered around the dinner table." Or my "Came home early from the ministers' conference to make my favorite boy a birthday cake." For five years, I parented four kids, not my usual two. Now, I haven't seen them in years.

When I first met Maggie, one of the things that drew me to her was how much she loved her children. Carter, her eight-year-old son, with enormous brown eyes and long lashes, and Casey, her adorable six-year-old daughter, were the lights of her life.* My own daughters, Mika, then eleven, and Marcella, who was nine, loved "the Cs" instantly, and we had great family times making snow people, drinking hot cocoa, and eating chocolate chip pancakes. We'd go together to the pumpkin patch and to watch Carter's baseball games. The kids got along great, always begging for sleepovers. We moved in together a year and a half after we met.

Because Maggie worked long and varied shifts four days a week, I often took her kids to school or picked them up. I look a great deal like one of Maggie's sisters, and her kids looked like they could have been mine. We went together to all of Carter's baseball and basketball games and Casey's softball games. I tucked them in at night, lying down and spinning original stories with prompts they'd give, and singing 70s pop tunes as lullabies.

---

* "Maggie," "Carter," and "Casey" are pseudonyms.

Our wedding was a joyful celebration of family. We made vows to the kids and had hula hoops and bubbles as part of the outdoor reception, which featured a pie potluck. The girls wore matching blue dresses and Carter wore a blue shirt and grey slacks, like his mother. We were each accompanied down the aisle by our children—me to "Ode to Joy," and Maggie to the Imperial March, Darth Vader's theme music. Perhaps that should have been a sign . . .

Maggie was a powerful force. When she was up, she pulled all of us into her joyous adventures. We'd make up silly games where we'd see how many advertising jingles everyone could remember, and go on surprise road trips and family hikes. We'd eat turkey tacos and then all curl up on the couch for movie nights, or play Ticket to Ride sprawled out across the floor.

But we all had to tiptoe around her moods. She particularly had little patience with Marcella. I had taught my kids that if I said no to something, the best way to get me to change my mind was with reasoned discussion, but Maggie read that as back-talk. My kids were in a stage where everything had to be fair—and so when Casey would report her miniature golf score as three, when we saw her hit the ball seven times, Marcella claimed that wasn't fair, and Maggie's insistence that Marcella could lie too didn't appease her at all.

Less than three years later, we divorced. Over time, Maggie had grown ever more impatient with me, and with Marcella. The girls and I began to do more things separately, and Marcella and Casey were arguing a lot. It was hard to not be loyal to our own children. The final straw, maybe, was a trip Maggie and I had planned to take with the three younger kids to Disneyland—one of Maggie's favorite places—but things were so tense at that point that Marcella and I both opted out. I don't think Maggie forgave me for that. Mika loved Maggie, and was very sad to leave, but it became clear that it wasn't a healthy atmosphere for Marcella anymore. Ultimately, I had to protect my child, and so we left.

I had hoped to stay in touch with Carter and Casey after the divorce. I'd watched them grow, driven miles in the minivan to baseball tournaments and school pickups. I'd spent long hours in lawn chairs and bleachers watching them play, and celebrated their successes and dried their tears. I'd showed up for their school activities, cooked them dinners and birthday cakes, and sung them to sleep, and I couldn't imagine not having them in my life. I sent them birthday cards and money for the first few years, until Maggie suggested that my gifts weren't landing well.

These last few years, I've realized that although I've run into Casey a couple of times over the years (and she's seemed glad to see me), I haven't seen Carter since he was thirteen and shorter than I was. Boys often look really different after puberty, and I was afraid I wouldn't recognize him, a thought that made me incredibly sad.

Carter graduated this past spring, and I watched the video of his high school commencement ceremony online. There were candid photos from the ceremony, and one was of a very tall young man with a mop of brown curls and dark brown eyes showing above a mask. The same eyes that look so like my own. I still ache to reconnect sometime, but I take some comfort in knowing that at least I'd recognize this child that, for so long, was one of my own.

When It's Quiet

REBEKAH A. SAVAGE

I remember the first night my children were not under my roof, but under their father's, after our separation and divorce. I came home after dropping them off, and as the door closed, I sank to the floor and just cried. It was too quiet. No little voices clamoring for dinner, no *Odd Squad* or *Daniel Tiger's Neighborhood* blaring from the TV room, no little hands tugging at my shirt for a drink or a hug. It was so quiet. I remember feeling as if I had lost a part of my identity, a part of myself in that quiet. My children were not home with me, and there was a hole in my heart, even bigger than the hole in my home.

I remembered when they each came home from the hospital. Tiny, precious humans entrusted to my care. I stared at them in wonder: "How can I be *your* parent?" These small sparks of life with their eyes searching my face for comfort, for love, for reassurance. These tiny hands reaching for me when the world was scary or felt too big. I was always a "we" back then, with two little humans encircling me like electrons in orbit. And they each had their own temperament: one who observed the world with a quiet curiosity and deep, pensive mind, and another who never met a stranger and was fearless in trying new things and meeting new people. When they were small children, we had so much fun together. I am the kind of parent that said Yes to going to the grocery store late on a Friday night in our PJs because we wanted ice cream. Yes to buying a brass lantern at the community garage sale and then going on "lantern walks" with the flame burning bright to guide our way on a dark path.

Yes to jumping off the top of my car into eight feet of snow during Snowmageddon with such glee each and every time. They were my constant soundtrack, my music and muse. My true delight.

So when their father and I divorced, the quiet was stunning and broke my heart. I tried to fill it with other activities and keep to a schedule: long runs, cooking from scratch, new DIY projects, and making our new home cozy and ours. Once I walked the seven miles to my office at church, just because I had time and I could. I trained for marathons because long runs were cathartic. I took a Nigerian cooking class and learned how to make vegetarian jollof. It was the quiet that got to me. When that door first closes and I realize I am alone in my home, *our home*, and my children are not there, that took some time to adjust to. Just as they have had to adjust to living in both my home and their father's home.

What I learned from that time is something I imagine "empty nesters" go through just a little bit later in their parenting than I did. I was pushed to find a bigger life, with an expanded identity that didn't involve taking care of my wonderful children 24/7. And now, after almost nine years of them being home with me a week at a time, the quiet is less haunting and they are moving towards being teenagers. I love them fiercely for who they are becoming. We have new rituals and ways of reconnecting when they return to me. And I am grateful for this journey and for how Love shows up still and always, crashing through the door each time they come home.

Witnessing Grace

PEGGY CLARKE

When my son was five, he and I were getting ready for another busy day when he pointed to a bird outside our window. On top of a maple tree sat a blue heron. We were on the second floor of the house and the tree is down a bit of a slope, putting this gorgeous bird directly in front of us.

Have you seen a blue heron? From head to tail they can be as much as five and a half feet, with a wing span up to seven! Slowly she extended her neck, with the grace of a seasoned ballerina. She was elegant and still, but so large we wondered how the branches could hold her; how was it they weren't buckling beneath her weight? She was light, balancing effortlessly, and the leaves nestled in around her.

I considered leaving the room to find my camera but didn't want to miss a moment. Zac must have felt the same way. In response to her tranquility, he and I stood equally still, watching her. Together we were caught in a bubble of silence that was rarely part of our morning routine. It was as though, if we moved, we'd frighten her, although there was no way she could see us. So we remained still and quiet.

Gracefully, she spread her wings and flew above the trees, long legs reaching behind her. Within moments, we lost sight of her. She flew behind the trees. On our way out, we stopped at the pond on our property, assuming we'd find her fishing for breakfast, as herons—blue, white, and even green—sometimes do, but she wasn't there. We waited a moment, thinking she was hiding, but she was gone. Her presence was brief, the way magic often is.

Love isn't always about two people gazing at each other. Often, it's about standing beside someone, witnessing the world together.

Diaper Wisdom

CHRISTIAN SCHMIDT

When one of my sons was quite young, no longer a baby but only just into toddlerhood, we were out at the local park. He was having a blast, though I noticed he was walking a little funny. He had, not for the first time, wet his diaper and right through his clothes, despite having a fresh diaper on. Such is life.

After all, I was prepared. I had the diaper bag, I had plenty of diapers and wipes, I had a change of clothes, I had a portable changing pad, I had everything! There was no public restroom nearby, but I made do: on a park bench, I laid him down on the pad, pulled off his little outfit, cleaned him up and got him in a brand-new diaper, ready to conquer the world! Off he went, toddling around the playground.

Except that almost immediately he returned, another wet stain spreading down his pants. I picked him up, wondering what on earth could have gone wrong. A quick investigation revealed the issue: I had failed to make sure his penis was completely inside the diaper, which it turns out almost completely stymies the diaper's capacity to hold fluid. And it gets worse! For all my preparations, it turned out I had packed only one spare outfit. All I could find in the bottom of the diaper bag was a shirt four sizes too big for him.

I felt awful. We had only just gotten to the park and now we would have to go home, which I knew my little boy would throw a fit about. So I did it. I put him in a fresh new diaper (triple-checked for proper placement) and dressed him in one ridiculously large shirt, and sent him off into the world. Off he went, in his giant t-shirt, happy as he could be. And I breathed several sighs of relief, relaxing on the park bench like I had just run a marathon.

I've since thought that there's a lesson in here for all of us (other than the obvious one, which is to make sure you tuck your penis into your clothing!). You can make all the preparations in the world. You can have all the experience. You can do (almost) everything right, and still, one little mistake can ruin the whole endeavor. Or, and stay with me here, you can be thankful for what you have and keep on playing.

Much of parenting has been like this for me: learning and growing and adjusting my expectations, many of which I never realized I had until they were broken. We have the child we have, not the one we might have planned for. We are the parent we are, not the parent we might wish we were. We can let those truths haunt us, or we can keep on playing. For my son, the choice was obvious. I'm still learning to be more like him.

Bad Parenting Award

Jane Rzepka

We wanted to expose our kids to the unimaginable. The point would be to clobber ourselves with majesty, to feel awed, to stretch ourselves, while scooting up and down mountainsides and across rope bridges. And so our family went trekking in the Himalayas.

We left roads behind, and anything level. As the days went on, we gave up notions of scooting along this challenging trail. The hiking was hard! Even so, the majesty lay before us, and the sense of awe.

But then our sixth grader, Toby, got amoebic dysentery. So did I. We were not just a little bit sick, but the kind where you languish in the tent, unable to eat. We lost a lot of weight while lying there staring at the peak of Ama Dablam through the tent flap.

The thing was, at a certain point, languishing any longer was not an option. For complicated logistical reasons, we needed to move forward on the trail. At least I thought so—Toby figured we'd just turn around and go home. But I was the mom, so Toby and I ventured forth with the rest of the family, me ever strategizing about how to make our feet move, one in front of the other. I settled on this: We took one hundred steps, and then allowed ourselves to rest. And another hundred. Rest. And another hundred. Until we found a villager who gave us some blackish mystery pills, which we eagerly swallowed.

I ask you, what parent does that, forces a child to hike in Very Big Mountains while so sick? And gives him odd-colored pills that could be anything? What parent can't even muster encouraging words, perspective, or amusement? Well, me.

The perfect experience we'd curated for our family did not work out as planned. Of course it didn't! Sometimes I stink at parenting— that's just the way it goes. And will go on going.

Toby and I recovered, of course, and even he would agree that our hundreds of steps, born of grit and perseverance, led us to astounding destinations high in the mountains. Toby was a good sport, and Ama Dablam remains etched in our memories. Yet part of me will always feel a little queasy when I think of that sick little boy gamely counting to a hundred, time and time again.

Our Funny Valentine

PARISA PARSA

My husband Enrique and I both grew up cross-culturally. Enrique was born in Chile and spent the early part of his life moving between the U.S. and Santiago. I was born in Iran and spent the early part of my life moving between the U.S. and Shiraz, Iran. When we met, we could hardly believe the similarities in our biographies, though the names of the places were different. Our families finally settled in the U.S. around the same time: Enrique's in suburban Boston in 1980; mine in mid-Ohio in 1979. We immigrated early enough in our lives to speak unaccented English and blend into U.S. culture fairly well. But we found that we shared odd moments of confusion at cultural things we had either missed entirely or misunderstood in our early upbringing. Those moments still happen as we co-parent children who are growing up "all-American."

Our son Kian had just begun at a Montessori preschool when Valentine's Day arrived. Kian had turned three just the month before. We had never celebrated Valentine's Day in our home, and I remembered having a passing question in my mind about whether it was a holiday celebrated in preschool. I dismissed the idea quickly, reasoning that it was ridiculous for preschoolers to celebrate what I took to be a romantic holiday. Besides, if there was some expectation, surely the school would have let us new parents know in advance, right?

When Enrique and Kian came to my office to pick me up that afternoon, Kian was sitting in his booster seat examining the Valentines he received at school that day. "This one is from Hana, this one from Zachariah ..." He held in a little brown bag Valentines from each and every child in his class. He had memorized which was from whom.

I was mortified, angry, confused. Thinking Kian was fully immersed in his Valentine inventory in the back seat, Enrique and I began a conversation. Neither of us understood, when there was so much sensitivity about holidays like Christmas, why there wasn't some information sent out about Valentine's Day. Then we began to recall our confusion about the holiday when we first experienced it upon moving to the U.S., and our own independently formed and collectively reinforced position that Valentine's Day is a silly holiday we neither understand nor support. But we were still embarrassed that our son was the only one who hadn't taken Valentines into class when it was clearly expected. For each of us, that brought up unpleasant memories of our own misfit status when we arrived; this was not an experience we wanted to pass along to Kian. We were not as assimilated as we thought we were; certainly not enough to protect him from what we had experienced ourselves as children. We thought we had said this quietly and moderately enough, as Kian continued saying out loud which card was from whom and singing to himself.

The next morning, as we were getting into the car to take Kian to school, he ran quickly back into the house and fetched his bag of Valentines. He insisted on bringing them in the car with him to school, though I explained repeatedly that they were his to keep. I thought perhaps another inventory was in order; thought he wanted them just for the ride. But then he insisted on taking them into school with him too. I dropped him off, clutching his little brown sack of notes like his life depended on it, and watched him trot into preschool.

No sooner had I arrived in my office that morning than I received a panicked call from Kian's teacher.

"I'm so sorry, I had no idea ..." Her words were coming out faster than the thoughts were forming and she was beside herself. I had no idea what she was talking about. Finally, I got her calmed down enough to understand what had happened.

"Kian marched right up to me with his bag of Valentines and said, 'I have to give these back. We don't celebrate Valentine's Day in my house.'"

When she insisted that it was okay to keep them, he refused outright. She knew I was a minister and assumed that there was some religious reason we didn't celebrate the holiday. She was mortally embarrassed, thinking she and the school had terribly offended us. I had to assure her that not only had she not offended us, but even if she had we would not have sent our three-year-old in to explain it to her.

I hung up the phone and called Enrique and we both sobbed. It was too much to bear. Not only had Kian picked up on far more of the conversation than we ever could have imagined; he had made a heartbreaking sacrifice. He adored those Valentines, each and every one, symbols of his new friends in preschool. The picture of him marching up to his bewildered teacher holding out the well-loved paper sack and giving them all up out of loyalty to us was more than we could bear. So was the thought that we had ruined that thrill and enjoyment for him with a conversation we so wrongly assumed was private. We were humbled twice over.

Aside from our profound lesson in the fact that (as my mother sometimes would say) "little pitchers have big ears," our hearts were pierced by a bittersweet new understanding of how one so new to the world could grasp the complex dimensions of love. How was it that this child, at the age of three, had managed to determine his own sense of loyalty, decide concern for our feelings was more important than his own enjoyment of the cards and sweets and gifts of friendship he so clearly adored, and determine to act on that? Kian had done all of this before we even were aware he was taking any of our conversation in. Meanwhile, our job as parents now was to make sure he knew that we would always want him to embrace and enjoy even the things we might not like or understand in the same way. That our love for him included letting him find and embrace his own experiences and understanding of this country, of this world, of life.

We all learned a lot about love that day.

Harbors

MARTA I. VALENTÍN

There is a deep sadness I've been harboring for a long time, but more so since I've moved out of parish and into community ministry. What began as a great joy when I found this faith, one that might flow into new generations, now weighs on me as a deep sadness.

In my first ministry, amid Hurricane Katrina's aftermath, my wife gave birth to our only child. The small but hardy and determined group of parishioners were thrilled that a new life would soon be joining our church community and they could help care for our baby. Yet for my wife and me, the impending birth was a signal it was time to move on. After Katrina flooded the childcare centers, people were surviving with the help of their families and friends, neither of which we had locally. We had arrived in New Orleans just the year prior but, due to the flooding and upheaval, our lives and those of the congregants were completely entwined. We also knew we did not want to raise our child in a recovery zone. Inviting congregants to cross the very personal boundary of caring for our child was not an option for us. What was an option was to leave, and it was heartbreaking to know we had that choice, but many whose lives were rooted in New Orleans did not. I allowed myself to be comforted by the notion that at least the congregation had a support system in each other that, as the newly arrived minister, I did not. The decision to leave would be the first among many difficult decisions I would make in favor of my child, her well-being, and her spiritual and religious education. Becoming a human shield against the racial, ethnic, and cultural microaggressions that would assail her like mosquito bites in this faith, upon which I placed my heart, would be at once the easiest and hardest decision.

At first, as a Latinx minister in a predominantly white congregation, I could keep an eye on what was happening to my daughter and other Black, Indigenous, or person of color (BIPOC) children and run interference when needed. Working with the congregation and staff as we strove toward creating an anti-racist, anti-oppressive, multicultural (ARAOMC) religious community enabled me to have some sway—in other words, to teach. But as my BIPOC ministerial colleagues can attest, life gets complicated very quickly when fending off microaggressions, whether to myself or to our children, by well-meaning congregants. While it's true that my wife was involved in my daughter's church upbringing too, and was there when I was in the sanctuary or a meeting, the situation was also complicated by expectations of her both as the minister's wife, and as a white person expected to uphold white supremacy (however subconscious that expectation may have been). We wanted our daughter to be raised in a faith community that accepted us wholeheartedly, but, as many BIPOC that come through our church doors know, reconciling the theology that brought us in with the cultural aspects formed by a majority white community is exhausting. It tends to go only one way: we have to adjust who we are, individually and as families. And while not all churches are the same, culture is culture, so there are only degrees of difference. There is no complete shift to saying, "All of who you are is valued and welcomed here."

So my sadness lives in the place of a ministry journey that, while it has had its moments of triumph and feeling right, has been challenging in ways I never could have imagined when I placed my heart on its altar. The inconsistent reality that belies who we say we are (and what we believe in) creates unsafe spaces for BIPOC folx and families, who, ironically, are often who we clamor to include, however haphazard or unrefined the attempt may be.

My sadness resides in the knowledge that although we *know* our young people leave us in droves, there doesn't seem to be a consistently concerted effort to keep them. I am aware of the pre-existing conditions that have made it difficult to keep youth engaged in local communities; an overarching belief is that "youth just do this." I am aware too of the amazing cadre of religious educators who have fought against this tide of our young people leaving, despite being (not just "feeling") unsupported. I am grateful for the current efforts to reverse this trend. Yet when I take it to a personal level, what I wonder the most in the deep quietness within me is this: How does a BIPOC religious professional justify raising their child or children in this faith, given what we have faced as adults in the system? Do I sacrifice my daughter's religious and spiritual development the way I have sacrificed myself for "the cause" of making this faith accountable, making it be who and what it proclaims itself to be?

My sorrow has deepened as I witness the lives of the few BIPOC young people we've known who are no longer hanging out with us, who perceive and have experienced us adults as hypocrites. It lives in the number of preacher's kids and children of other religious professionals, who arguably receive the "training" more profoundly, turning away from this faith and the heartache that it causes within families.

I wonder: Am I about to face this too? I can already see the signs in my own daughter, and I do not think they are pandemic related, although I am sure current circumstances are making the exit more enticing. Now fourteen, she has grown up in two churches she has loved, but she now sees for herself just how "minoritized" we are. She has witnessed and lived the consequences of my ministerial journey in this faith, as much as I tried to shield her. In one of the churches

I was the minister, so the need to be accountable was clearly in congregants' face all the time. In the second church, I am in the pews, virtual as they may be right now. I have entered in good faith, but also during these last few years the deeper reality of BIPOC people's lives and deaths has caused me to reflect on my own life: Where am I? What am I doing here? Why am I here? Do I have the energy to move them toward justice work so that I can feel like I belong?

Toward the end of my sporadic church appearances before the pandemic, the silence grew louder at coffee hour as I stood alone, repeating the same questions: Is it because I intimidate by being a minister in their midst, or because I am one of a handful of BIPOC adults and children (although some people may be unaware either that I am ordained or that I am Latinx)? I grow tired of being the proactive one, the one going toward another; I long for the reverse. It is difficult to say this out loud to my longtime ministerial colleague, and to my wife, who can now be a board member since coming out of the shadowed identity of "the minister's wife." The lack of movement along the ARAOMC continuum that she witnessed earlier, when I was the leader, she now feels more deeply as she attempts to co-lead the effort.

My sadness grows in the urgency that I feel to save my BIPOC daughter and others like her who are awakening to the injustices in the world and are seeing the discrepancies within their faith communities. Who have ideas for how our faith can move forward, but who don't know how to advocate or, if BIPOC, are busy educating their peers, who often think they *are* educated on the social justice issues of today. This anguish rears its broken heart when I start to feel that I will be trapped if I and my family remain in this faith. I can't imagine leaving this faith after all I've put into it, but I also don't want to feel, as I do sometimes, that I am stuck in it. I know of other BIPOC folx who characterize their life in this faith as having one foot in and the other out, always on a threshold. But my daughter is just beginning, and I want her to be a part of a faith community, knowing that in the end, if she chooses to stay, it will be for her own reasons.

My profoundest sadness is that there is a huge potential for history to repeat itself, instead of building on itself. I left the Catholic Church, much to my devout mother's disappointment, when as a lesbian I felt there was no space for me. But I was hoping that I was growing a new branch on the spirituality tree in our family, so that one day in the future my child's offspring would say, as a BIPOC among many BIPOCs, "I'm third generation born and bred," as they introduced their family into a church community where many people looked like them.

Jesus Christ Superstar

AISHA HAUSER

My children grew up listening to the soundtrack of *Jesus Christ Superstar*. They found the story of the life and death of Jesus of Nazareth fascinating. This in and of itself would not be of interest, except that my children were born of a Muslim-raised mother and Jewish-raised father and for three years attended a Catholic school. This laid the groundwork for some interesting exchanges over the years between us.

One of these exchanges occurred after we watched the 1973 movie version of *Jesus Christ Superstar*. My son, Luke, who was four years old at the time, turned to me and asked, "Why did the Romans kill Jesus, Mommy?" I initially tried explaining the politics of the time, but quickly realized that they were way over his head. He would look at me puzzled when I even tried. He then turned to the idea of God. "Mommy, is God in the trees? Is God in the water? Is God in bad people?"

All of these are straightforward questions to a four-year-old, but as an adult who sometimes struggles with these same questions, especially the one about God and "bad people," I was stumped on how to answer. At some point, I realized I was overthinking the need to answer them; that what he really wanted was reassurance, and not a dissertation on the existential nature of our search for an all-powerful deity to allay our fears of what happens when we die. When I finally let go of wanting the "right answer," I simply told him that, yes, God was in the trees, in the water, and even in "bad people." His follow-up question (at four, he *always* had follow-up questions) was, why would God be in "bad people" and why would they stay "bad"? After a deep sigh, and taking a moment to respond, I finally landed on an imperfect response, but one that seemed to satisfy him for a while, at least. I told him that even though I believe that God is love and goodness, sometimes people don't listen to the goodness inside of them, for many reasons: sometimes they are afraid, or have been hurt. They become unkind and do things that hurt others, rather than listening to the God inside them.

My children are now young adults, and their questions and observations about God have evolved and become nuanced. I will not share where they are on their spiritual journeys, as those are their stories to tell. I will share that I learned from them how to be open to humble curiosity about the beliefs others hold, not be attached to having someone think or feel the same way I do about what God is or isn't. And together we still wonder about the big questions Luke raised, the ones with no easy (or entirely satisfying) answers: how so much pain and suffering is caused by those who choose to inflict harm on others; where God is in all of this; and how we find our way to love, healing, wholeness, and holiness in the midst of it.

We Bring Food

EMILY GAGE

A while ago, our family was on a doorstep, waiting for someone to open the door to our ring. We had brought them a meal. Quietly, before they answered, my five-and-a-half-year-old son turned to me and said, "Did someone die?"

He did not know who we were delivering a meal to, but he did know this. In times of sadness and crisis, we bring food.

He knows this because when his Grammy died, we went to a memorial service at her church, and afterwards, everyone sat down to a meal together. Food had been provided and served by many, many hands, and many more hands assured that we got seconds, and cleaned up, and let us sit and grieve and share stories. He knows this because afterwards, people brought food to our house so we didn't have to cook.

Some of this was about the food, of course. But it was mostly about kindness. Poet Naomi Shihab Nye, in her poem "Kindness," writes, "Before you know what kindness really is, you must lose things."

The day of his Grammy's funeral and the days that followed, I knew what Nye meant. When we lose someone we love, or experience any loss—of a physical ability, a job, or a relationship—and we receive some sort of kindness in those times, we are so open-heartedly vulnerable that I do think we truly know what kindness means.

And in the moment we were delivering food, at that friend's doorway, I was reminded how sometimes good things are about a kind of loss too.

It happened that our son arrived as a total surprise. We got a call that he was ours on a Tuesday and brought him home on a Thursday. We had nothing for him in our house. Literally *nothing*. But our neighbors brought a bassinet for him to sleep in. People in our congregation chipped in and bought us a stroller. Piles of tiny clothes found their way to our house. There was soup waiting for us in the kitchen freezer. My sister got on a plane to come and help. And all of it was partly about food and diapers and the bazillion little things that you immediately need, even if only for a very short period of time, to care for an infant. But it was mostly about kindness.

A new baby, even when it is the most wanted thing in the world, is also a kind of loss. At the very least it is a loss of a different kind of life. My recollection of those first weeks of being a parent are kind of a haze, as I coped with disorientation, lack of sleep, and wonder that this tiny being, born prematurely, was depending on us. It was hard, gorgeous, and scary, all of it. And I do not recall being particularly articulate. And I recall myself dazedly receiving all kinds of gestures of kindness. I was and am in awe of the generosity of spirit that surrounded us. It mattered.

It was these sorts of kindnesses that helped create healing. All those loving hands helped nurture us as we found our way into a new way of being. It was that care—intimate, and practical too sometimes—that reminded us that we were not alone, and connected us to one another and, in the deepest ways, to what it means to be human.

That particular day when our family stood on the steps of a house, ringing the bell, we were delivering food to another family— one with a new baby. Because our family has learned that in times of new life and joy, just as in times of pain, we bring food (or whatever else is needed). Because loss comes in a lot of forms. And healing and nurture are needed in a lot of circumstances. And kindness, when it comes down to it, is not about fixing things. So much cannot be fixed or changed.

Kindness is about understanding and accompanying someone when hard things happen. It's about bringing food.

Love's Pronoun Is Plural

ELEA KEMLER

My son, Caleb, and I went to Starbucks on a recent Saturday morning. We often do this as a prelude to the weekly grocery shopping. It sweetens the deal, which is important, as he is about to be fourteen and is on the autism spectrum. Both of these factors contribute to his resistance to what in the autism world we call "non-preferred activities." Caleb is really tall for his age, 6'4" and still growing. This is a factor because he is big and often gets in people's way without realizing. He is also a sweet, sensitive kid, which is not a factor, except that I am his mother.

Caleb was standing by the counter, waiting for his Frappuccino (decaf—we don't want to stunt his growth) and blocking the path of a young dad trying to herd three small children. The dad said to Caleb, "Could you get your head out of the clouds and get out of the way." It was not horrible, just frustrated and a little unkind, something a person says when they think other people's kids are being rude. Something a person says when they haven't learned there are disabilities you can't immediately see.

Fortunately, Caleb remained oblivious, but I walked over to the dad and said to him quietly, "He's on the autism spectrum. He doesn't know where his body is in space or when he's in someone's way." I did not add, though I wanted to, "You may not realize this yet, but I promise you that someday your children will also need the kindness of strangers."

Soon it will be Caleb's decision whether or not to explain himself. But as he gets older and bigger (and bigger), my fear gets bigger too. I fear he will be met with more judgment and less understanding. He is so easily hurt; I fear the meanness. The dad nodded. He did not say anything but I thought maybe he took it in, a little bit.

We ended up sitting at the counter next to another young dad and his daughter. That dad told Caleb in great detail about the Clover coffee machine they now have at Starbucks and how it works and why the coffee it makes is better. They talked about pistons and forced hot water for a long time. "Thank you," I told him, when Caleb got up to go to the bathroom. "My son is on the spectrum too," he said. We smiled at each other and I remembered again that we are never alone, even when fear tells us we are. I remembered again that I choose to trust in kindness. I choose to believe that my child will not be alone either.

Life So Sacred

Sarah Gibb Millspaugh

The week after I gave birth to my son Maxfield Isaiah, the Iraq War—"Operation Iraqi Freedom"—came to an official close. It had already been several years since George W. Bush swooped in and declared "mission accomplished." After 162,000 traumatic deaths, including 4,000 children,* the eight-year-long, deceitfully conceived war was finally ending.

One hundred and sixty-two thousand deaths. I spell that out, because even now, I can't quite take it in. One hundred and sixty-two thousand deaths. How can we even fathom the pain of that many lives traumatically lost? We who grew up with numbers rolling off tongues, like "six million Jews" or "a hundred thousand in Hiroshima and Nagasaki," we who have perhaps grown immune to immense tallies of the dead . . . how could we even know the extent of what we had done?

So there I sat as I cradled and rocked my newborn son, a child so tender that just a fall to the floor could be catastrophic, and clung to his new life while I listened to retrospectives on the Iraq War on NPR, and I felt not only my love for my son but deeply sad and very angry. I had worked so hard to keep this war in Iraq from happening. Local demonstrations and marches on Washington, letters to Congress and pleas to the president. Despite the largest worldwide protests in history, Bush, Cheney, Rumsfeld, and Wolfowitz had plotted on.

---

* Iraq Body Count, "Iraqi Deaths from Violence, 2003-2011," January 2, 2012, www.iraqbodycount.org/analysis/numbers/2011/.

I remembered March 20, 2003, the official first day of the war. A graduate student in theology, I was preparing to serve a faith that proudly promotes "the inherent worth and dignity of every person." That day I left grad school classes to march through the streets of Cambridge and into Boston in protest.

As I marched, I remember seeing a boy, just eleven or twelve years old, standing with a group of pro-war counter-protestors. The sandy-haired, round-faced boy held a big homemade sign with a picture of a military jet on it, and "Get Saddam" written below.

It was not my habit to engage counter-protestors, but before I even realized what I was doing, I blurted out to the boy, "Do you know that our bombs won't just 'get' Saddam? They'll kill innocent kids like you. Do you want that?" The boy stared at me, stunned, and I walked on.

On December 15, 2011, the official last day of the war, a different boy was staring at me, and he wasn't looking away. My baby Maxfield was just a week old, a floppy little newborn, capable of nursing and sleeping, crying, and looking around. He was so helpless on his own. My husband and I had been up with him, every hour or two, all night every night since his birth.

As I rocked and listened, I heard story after story about the Iraq war coming to an end, stories that attempted to take stock of the nearly nine years of violence. Tears began to well in the corners of my tired eyes. And then they wouldn't stop. This war had been an utter travesty and an unfathomable tragedy.

And no doubt because I fed and rocked my sweet newborn as I listened to all this, it hit me even more deeply. These lives, each life of an Iraqi soldier, and child, mother, grandparent . . . Each life of an American soldier and contractor . . . Each life . . . Every person started out as a tiny, helpless, and extraordinarily dear baby.

I looked down at my son. His deep sacredness was so evident, right there in his restless baby body. Every hardened soldier, every enemy combatant, every ISIS-in-Iraq fighter . . . they had all been babies. I'd known this mentally, but with my own baby in my arms I somehow literally felt it: every person came into the world in this way. Every person. Tiny and helpless. Whether we were born into a loving home or not, someone had to take care of each of us, tending and feeding us through the days and through the nights, or we never would have made it. Each of us was so precious as a baby.

And the tears just flowed—sadness, anger, rage. All the deaths and serious injuries and the trauma of loss to hundreds of thousands of people. All this life, so sacred and so vulnerable. "When did they ever stop being sacred, or cease to be so precious?" I kept asking myself. "When did that ever stop?"

Through my tears, the truth, the answer to my question, crystallized. It is this: none of us has ever stopped being as sacred as a baby—this baby. The God I believe in imbues each life with a holiness, an integrity, a worth that persists throughout our lives, no matter what we have done. None of us is more valuable than another. Each one of those lives lost and shattered was as worthy as my child's life, or my own. There in the rocking chair, I cried for the tragedy and the truth that were revealed in the haze and clarity of being a newborn's mother.

The prophet Isaiah, whose name we had just given as a middle name to our sweet baby son, asked,

> Can a woman forget her nursing child,
> or show no compassion for the child of her womb?
> Even these may forget, yet [God] will not forget you.
> (Isaiah 49:15, NRSV)

I give thanks for the emotionally permeable state I was in after giving birth, because it made room for a spiritual reality to anchor within me. A spiritual reality that my Universalist faith has proclaimed for two and a half centuries, but that each person may need to come to know in their bones in their own way. A truth that we are all beloved children of God. All siblings, kin. All sacred. That each of us deeply matters in the most unshakable of ways.

I had marched on the first day of the war because I believed, profoundly, in the inherent worth and dignity of every person. But on that last day of the war, I could *feel* it.

Today, despite that moment of knowing, it is still a daily struggle to live out this sacred truth. We are all caught up in systems that regularly assign more worth to some lives, and consider others to be disposable. Simply by driving our cars, shopping to get the best deal, or paying our taxes, we empower entities that quietly reinforce the fundamental assumption that some people's lives inherently don't count as much as the comfort or convenience of the powerful.

As my son has grown, I've invited him to share this struggle with me and his dad, yet it rarely feels like enough. He goes to protests with our family, moving from chanting "Black Lives Matter!" as a preschooler to holding up a "No Detention for Kids" sign outside an immigration jail as an elementary schooler. He's been an active participant in our conversations and then choices about how to show up in movements for justice. He knows what our family stands for and he has the beautiful ability to articulate his own spiritual values. Right now, he is outraged that any life would be considered more valuable, or less valuable, than any other. He seems to know in his bones the spiritual truth that he taught me all those years ago. And our job as parents seems to be to help make sure he doesn't forget it in the midst of the noise of a world that feels too bent on othering, diminishing, and deadening us to one another's full humanity and to all that our own full humanity demands of us.

That boy who wanted to "get Saddam" all those years ago—he is probably about thirty now, old enough to have held his own baby in his arms. I hope he realizes now that he and his family were mistaken about invading Iraq, especially given all that followed. My prayer for him, and for all of us who sometimes forget, is that he may come to know unmistakably the spiritual truth of our infinite sacredness, maybe while he holds his young child someday, or sings to his dying grandparent, or is heartstruck by the suffering of a person halfway around the world whose story makes it to him and breaks him open to all those things that connect us. May he come to know that all lives count: all of us, our whole lives through. And may he feel the call to live and love and shape the world anchored in that sacred, life-giving, life-affirming place.

A Feminist, Newly Born

Manish Mishra-Marzetti

As an openly gay man of color, who has for many decades navigated political, societal, cultural, and religious structures that were never designed to include me, I have felt a strong kinship with feminism my whole adult life. The seeds of this commitment were planted in me in my childhood, by my witnessing the routine physical and emotional abuse my mother experienced as an Indian woman in a Hindu arranged marriage. The violence I saw her navigate was culturally justified through patriarchal norms: Indian women, in this highly conservative/traditional mindset, were an appendage to the men around them. A woman existed to be of service to the man she was attached to—whether father, brother, or husband—as all-purpose cook, cleaner, launderer, and intimate spouse; not in some outdated, bygone era such as the eighteenth or nineteenth century, but in the 1970s, 80s, and 90s.

I was driven to an innate sense of feminism out of disgust at the abuse I routinely saw directed at my mother: the ways in which she was treated like an object—something to be possessed and controlled—rather than as a human being with hopes, dreams, and aspirations of her own. As a result, I was clear: if the universe saw fit to gift my husband and me with a child that was biologically female, we would not foist upon that child colors, toys, clothing, stories, tropes, or anything else that limited that child's sense of possibilities. We would support that child in living into their fullest potential.

I was already clear, in my heart, about these commitments ... and then arrived the babe, a biologically female child. A gentle being, always smiling, always yearning for caring touch, interested in connection and relationship from the very beginning. It was striking how our Mina embodied in ways so tangible some of the qualities which in Hinduism are associated with *Shakti*, the divine feminine; Mina radiated love, more love, and in all ways the intuitive and creative possibilities of relationship. Within Hinduism, such energies are often associated with the goddess Saraswati, who represents the creative love of art, wisdom, and learning. Our family was blessed with a living embodiment of all these energies.

It was mid-2014, Mina was just a couple of months old, and the *Washington Post* ran an article about two teenage girls in my ancestral state of Uttar Pradesh, in India, who had been gang-raped and murdered; two of the accused were police officers. This was the latest report of such an assault I had read, following other accounts such as that of a solo female tourist being physically and sexually assaulted, and another of a young Indian woman being brutally raped on a crowded public bus, without anyone doing anything to stop it. The horrifying statistic that the *Washington Post* reported was that a woman is raped in India every twenty-two minutes—amidst criminal, legal, political, and social structures that often do nothing meaningful to transform the underlying attitudes and behaviors that tacitly create such violence. Multiple stories, multiple experiences of abhorrent human behavior, not decades earlier, but in the present day.

Yet, now, in mid-2014, my life was fundamentally different. This was the world that my baby—my innocent little baby—would inherit. These were the social realities that Mina's life, in all its beauty and possibility, would interact with. I could help my child be courageous. My husband and I could throw wide open the world of learning and help impart healthy boundaries. We could encourage Mina to unapologetically claim a rightful place in society; to delight in and develop innate gifts, and to offer them to a world needing more creativity and love. We could do what was possible for us to do, in nurturing a life that was different from the life my mother had, but this was a *world*—cultures, societies, peoples—that despite our efforts still disrespected and brutalized women. And, what that might mean for our dear, sweet Mina—only four months old—came flooding in.

I did, then, what I imagine many parents have done through time. With tears in my eyes, I went to my sleeping babe's crib and prayed:

Dear God, dear Universe, dear All-That-Is, please please let the men that this little life encounters be good, decent, and kind. Please. Just please. I'm begging you.

And I wept, and I wept, and I wept, painfully cognizant of all that I would never be able to control. At the same time, I could feel a quickening, a parallel birth of its own, taking shape within me—an even deeper, fiercer commitment to supporting the dignity of women.

Maybe the world is healed in this way: by the shaken, kneeling prayers of parents and loved ones, around the world, who in the midst of feeling powerless commit to doing what they can, wherever they can, in service to building a world of greater dignity for all.

Pandemic Journal Entry 201

ROBIN TANNER

I am staring at the driveway again and the little patch of green next to it. I am watching you play with the sand shovel as you desperately try to garden with the flimsy pink shovel made for softer earth, easier days.

What will I tell you, little one, of this time?

That we stayed together . . . that we screamed over burnt dinner and wept at our screams and had kitchen dance parties? That sleep was a distant memory, but your beautiful spirit made playing in the dirt mystical this day and forever in my mind? That we wiped down our groceries and panicked when we sneezed? That we snuck into your room to contemplate the next terror and the armor we could weld for you? That we looked at stars and studied each "futter-by" as if it was the Spirit herself descending on the tomato flower? That each dawn, no matter how reluctant we were, the birds sang us into being? That we noticed and noticed and fought and fought and leapt, we prayed, toward that for which we were made?

Yes, we will tell you and show you. Far beyond this day with the flimsy pink shovel, you will know that we planted, tended, and harvested something real for you. We woke each day and remembered, in the briefest of moments, staring at the little patch of green next to the driveway and your tender hands grasping the shovel handle . . . we remembered for what we were made. And together we kept moving toward that life and love.

Imani's Question

CHERYL M. WALKER

There used to be a television program called *Kids Say the Darndest Things*, in which children would say things that adults found cute and amusing. What there should also be is a show entitled *Kids Ask the Darndest Questions—And They Really Want Answers*. Anyone who has spent an appreciable amount of time with a four-year-old knows this to be true. Most times we adults give the best answer we can in the moment, and that seems to be satisfactory. If it is not, it will be followed by another question. And another, and another.

Sometimes, the question is more important to the adult than the answer is to the child. When my niece Imani (her name means *faith* in Swahili) was four she asked me such a question. Innocent on her part, it would be the most important question anyone ever asked me. The entire trajectory of my life changed because she asked "Imani's question."

It was going to be a lovely weekend with my sister and her children. We lived in different states but I made a point of visiting often so that I could be a part of her children's lives. My sister warned me before I came down that Imani was in the "death stage." She had discovered the concept of death and was eager to talk about it with anyone and everyone. I had been through this phase with my other niece and children of my friends, so I felt prepared this time.

Sure enough, we sat in the backyard and Imani said to me, "Grandpa died." My father had died not too long ago, and I replied, "Yes, I know."

85

"He died from candy," Imani said.

This was confusing, so I excused myself and asked my sister why Imani thought our father died of candy. My sister told me that she had told Imani that he died of cancer, rather than saying he died because he was sick. Having learned from her first child that such an explanation would mean every time someone got sick she would think they were going to die, my sister was more specific this time. Imani somehow confused cancer and candy, and because she no longer asked for candy as much—because it would kill you—my sister decided not to correct her.

I returned to my conversation with Imani.

"Auntie Cheryl, am I going to die?"

"Yes, Imani, one day a long time from now, you will die."

"Auntie Cheryl, are you going to die?"

"Yes, Imani, one day I will die. Someday everyone will die."

At this point I thought I was ready for the next question. After all, I'd been through this before. I was expecting Imani to ask, somewhat gleefully, as they all had, "Auntie Cheryl, when are you going to die?"

I had some answer prepared, which I do not remember anymore, so I felt ready. But "Imani" means *faith* and that is not the question she asked. Instead she asked, "Auntie Cheryl, how many more mornings will you wake up before you die?"

I was not prepared for *that* question. Imani waited patiently for an answer. After a bit I answered, "More than Maya can count." Maya is Imani's older sister, who was just shy of seven back then. I knew she could count to a hundred, but after that it got a little iffy.

It was a good enough answer for Imani, and she changed the subject to something else.

She was satisfied and I was left uneasy. How many more mornings would I wake up? What was I doing with those mornings? What should I be doing with those mornings? The question nagged at me and nagged at me. And the next thing I knew I was going to seminary. It changed my life forever, and the question stays with me still.

"How many more mornings will you wake up before you die?"

The Bed

MARLIN LAVANHAR

Assembling the bed,
screwdriver in hand,
he has no idea
what will transpire.

The sweat dripping from his brow
christens the wood slats
as he fits the pieces together:
A large rectangle
like the frame for a great picture
but more like a setting for a series
of pictures.

The bed will be like
a family album
containing page after page
of photos,
scenes from a life,
a series of lives.

With the tools still on the floor
he gets on the freshly made bed.
The sheets smell of lavender detergent.
The mattress responds to his body.
But not as delightfully as she does
when they make love on it
for the first time

or the thirty-first time.
A girl is conceived
on the bed.
The lovers still catching their breath
have no idea
the curtain has just opened
on the next act in the play
that is their family.

Months later,
in the bed,
more moans
and strong breathing.
This time it's mom
giving birth.
The midwife's hands
guiding a glistening baby girl
into the world,
onto the bed.

Now there are three of them
each night
lying together
breathing in and out.
There is so much love.
So little sleep.
Milk drips onto bodies,
onto the sheets.

The bed
that provides the canvas
for scene after scene
is indifferent to each event.

Indifferent to arguments
that happen between the sheets.
Indifferent to nausea and ecstasy.
The bed has no rules of its own
no expectations
no judgments.

When she lies breathless
on the bed
three days after her third birthday
the wailing rings out
from the mother
like a tornado siren

Conception, birth, death, grief;
the bed was indifferent to it all.

A place to start breathing and to stop
breathing.

A place to surrender,
to love,
in all its incarnations.

May 2, 2016
(Sienna's thirteenth birthday anniversary)

Veil

KIM WILDSZEWSKI

I have packed your favorite foods
a juice box with a bendy straw
and your coat in case it gets cold.

I am coming with my picnic basket
flowers, some books
and song.

I am ready, sweet beloved,
for the steel wall of Here
and There
to break into fine moveable metals.

For the dirt and earth and
whatever has made home in the ash of your body
to choose something less separate
again.

I am ready, sweet child,
for the veil to become thin.

If you were to reach out from your grave
like the children fear
I would reach back for you.

If you were to flash the lights
like the movies show
I would dance to the strobe light
of your spirit.

I sleep for your dream.
I wake for your memory.
I love and laugh and claim joy
in your honor.

I am ready, sweet beloved.
Here is your hat, your soft things,
the snow boots you wore all spring.

They say the veil
will thin.

Another, Truer Song

ELEA KEMLER

I first visited a children's psychiatric unit twenty-two years ago. The boy's mother and I stood facing each other in the hallway by the locked door, not saying a word because there was nothing to say. He was ten years old and seemed not to want to live. He had been putting belts and yo-yo strings around his neck. I reached toward her and put my hand on the flat plane just beneath her collar bones, the place where sadness collects in my own body. I was a new minister then, and guarding against such intimate gestures had not yet become a habit. Much later she told me it had helped: that in that moment she felt less like the only mother in the world who ever had a suicidal child.

I visited the boy every few days, getting buzzed in through the locked doors. Soon we had a routine of finding a quiet place on the floor to play chess and checkers. He beat me every game, partly because I had forgotten anything resembling strategy and also because I was paying more attention to the songs we sang while we played.

He began this musical conversation on the second visit—humming under his breath as he moved his pieces—and then he started adding words. Mostly, the words were about what was happening on the board. "I am going to juuuuummmp you," he sang.

"If I move like this, you cannot juuummmmp me," I sang back. I wondered if he was singing me another, truer song underneath, so I was listening carefully and trying to choose what to sing back.

"You are doomed; there is no way out," he sang, as he claimed another of my checkers.

"I am not doomed," I answered. "There is always another chance, as long as you will keep plaaaaaaying."

He never protested when I got ready to go but sometimes, as I walked him back to his room, he held my hand and leaned his head against my arm. On those days I cried in the parking lot. I wanted so much to believe that God was watching over this boy, that God was tender and protective and fiercely on the side of life and that this boy would not slip away.

Months later, after he left the hospital, the boy presented me with a combined game of chess and checkers during a church service. He told our congregation we had played a lot together when he was "in the hospital with sadness" and that he beat me every single time. "This game is for you, so you don't forget how to play," he told me.

The boy is a man now. He is married and has good work and two little ones of his own. He has not been lost and I have not forgotten.

Bit by Bit

KIM WILDSZEWSKI

While walking the overlit halls of Buy Buy Baby
I remembered the man who,
after his baby died,
took the crib to the end of the driveway
and smashed it
bit by bit.

You can't really pick up all those pieces.
Can't sweep the splinters or paint chips
from the soil and grass.

I'd bet a spring came loose in the fury.
I'd guess he didn't bother loosening
each rung from its screw before
dragging it outside.

All these decisions we make
From paint color to names
From dreams and a place of joy

As if the redwoods aren't burning
As if disease isn't spreading
As if marbles, grapes, guns, and
swimming pools without gates
don't exist.

You can't really pick up all those pieces
once the universe of a body

just stops.
Once loving begins to feel like
risk.

But here we are
walking the aisles of
Buy Buy Baby
with our hand sanitizer and masks
with our lists
and our lists of names.
Trying to decide on the color of
a crib

Carried Up to Bed

Elizabeth Lerner Maclay

Wouldn't we all wish to be carried up to bed one more time?

So dependent, so confident, and so cared for, in that particular way, for all the right reasons. We are not ill, nor hurt, nor helpless. We are simply small and tender and tired.

How long have parents carried their children to bed, have children enjoyed that passive bliss? There we lie, half-asleep already, in a car or on a sofa after a late night. We could be roused but our eyes are closed—we are less asleep than we look, more asleep than we feel.

Our parent comes to fetch us up to bed and slides a strong, quiet arm under our shoulders and neck, another under our knees, and hoists us up to be carried to our rooms and our waiting sheets. We sleepily turn toward them, maybe hike an arm loosely over their shoulder and around their neck and hang on a bit. We feel them walking down the hall, or stepping up the stairs, and then nudging open the door to our room, walking across the floor of the dark, familiar space. We know where we are without opening our eyes. We feel them pause by the bed to get a firmer grip, and then lean over and lay us down, pulling the sheets down to fold our legs in, pulling the sheets up to tuck us in.

Would that I had known that last time for what it was. Now it is my task to do the tender carry, the kiss and caress across the face before leaving the room. That is precious too. But, children, know the date-stamped preciousness of being carried up to bed for what it is and nestle into its warmth.

Years will pass and we will still feel small and tender and tired and this gift will likewise have passed, gone to others, to our own and others' children. And we will each of us have then only the memory and the charge to carry on tradition, the sweet burden, the carrying of another.

Almost Goodbye

VANESSA RUSH SOUTHERN

It must have been around six months, about when we were told it should happen, that our daughter, Leila, our only child, crawled across the living room rug for the first time. Rohit, my husband, and I were both there to see it, all that coordination of limbs, chubbiness in determined motion. We cheered, which was probably what made the kid fall over, and then I started crying—sobbing, I guess.

"What's the matter?" Rohit asked, surprised and confused, as one would be. And here's what I said, which is what I thought, in that moment of her first crawl through the universe: "Now she's crawling, then soon she'll be walking"—he nodding, with an expression of *Yes, so far so good, right?*—"and then she'll be leaving home and going to college and it will all be over."

It was jumping the gun, of course, but it was where my mind and heart went. That sense that time, once started, just blasts off and is over in an eye-blink.

There was a lot I didn't mention or foresee in that moment. The stuff that filled up the years: first days of this or that, illness and sleepovers, her decision to be a vegetarian, our moves, the ways she would change how she saw herself in the world and how others would respond to her and see her gifts, getting grit, being gutsy, being compassionate and a great dancer—oh, and all that constant singing in the house, that too. So much between crawling and leaving.

But Bean, as we call her, is seventeen now and a "rising senior," and I feel that same desire to cry, right up against the urgency and compulsion to "suck out all the marrow of life" or at least this chapter of it, to use Thoreau's words. I have already told some people that this year, being present for almost all family occasions will be my priority. It's my last chance to soak up this bit of life before it goes. And I have some things I need to do before I let her go out into the world without me right behind her.

But also, that woman crying, all those years ago, kneeling on the living room rug behind a surprised, chubby baby who just figured out how to make arm and leg work in opposing rhythm to propel her forward, she was right. They *were* just an eye-blink away from goodbye.

We Will Tell Them

ROBIN TANNER

There was grief, we will tell them, that appeared to swallow us up . . .
Fear that pounded in our brains and ran drip
Drip
Drip
At night . . .
There was loss stalking us like wolves at every corner.
And we will tell them
We
Not some mythical history maker
But we
Will tell them
How they singularly saved a day
Brought forth a reason to burn on
By putting one foot to a pedal
And pushing toward the possible.
How they reminded us
That things once impossible
Are not always so.
That the holy is here as we are haunted.
That it and we endured.
We will tell them.